T5-DIE-125

3 2711 00061 3200

APR '98

ENTERED DEC 3 0 1993

COLUMBIA COLLEGE
LIBRARY

RETENTION OF AFRICAN-AMERICAN MALES IN HIGH SCHOOL

A Study of African-American Male High School Dropouts, African-American Male Seniors and White Male Seniors

Annie S. Barnes
Norfolk State University

UNIVERSITY
PRESS OF
AMERICA

Lanham • New York • London

Copyright © 1992 by
University Press of America®, Inc.
4720 Boston Way
Lanham, Maryland 20706

3 Henrietta Street
London WC2E 8LU England

All rights reserved
Printed in the United States of America
British Cataloging in Publication Information Available

Library of Congress Cataloging-in-Publication Data

Barnes, Annie S.
Retention of African–American males in high school : a study of
African–American male high school dropouts, African–American male
seniors and white male seniors / Annie S. Barnes.
p.   cm.
Includes bibliographical references and index.
1. Afro–American dropouts—Virginia—Norfolk—Case studies.
2. Afro–American students—Virginia—Norfolk—Case studies.
3. High school students—Virginia—Norfolk—Case studies.   I. Title.
LC146.7.V8B37   1992   373.12'913'089960730755521—dc20
91–46304 CIP

ISBN 0–8191–8508–6 (cloth : alk. paper)

373.12913 B261r

Barnes, Annie S.

Retention of African-
American males in high

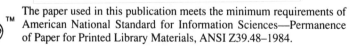

The paper used in this publication meets the minimum requirements of
American National Standard for Information Sciences—Permanence
of Paper for Printed Library Materials, ANSI Z39.48–1984.

ACKNOWLEDGMENTS

There are many people who have been directly or indirectly responsible for this book and I extend my apreciation to them. My special appreciation is expressed to Dr. Jesse C. Lewis, Vice President for Academic Affairs, Norfolk State University, Norfolk, Virginia, for helping initiate this project. My special appreciation is also expressed to Dr. Gene Carter, Superintendent of the Norfolk, Virginia Public Schools, who gave permission to conduct the study in the five Norfolk High Schools and among the high school dropouts. I also owe a debt of gratitude to Dr. Frank Sellew, an assistant superintendent, for his assistance, and to Dr. Anna Dodson, Director of the Norfolk Public Schools Department of Research, Testing and Statistics, and Mr. James Staton, Supervisor of Student Affairs in the Norfolk Public School System, for helping implement this study. Similarly, I owe a debt of gratitude to the principals of the five high schools who assisted data collection. They are Dr. Theodore Smith, Mr. Raleigh Baggett, Mr. James Slaughter, Mr. Claude Sawyer, and Dr. Thomas A. Newby.Also, my appreciation is extended to Mr. William Davis, Principal of the Norfolk Technical and Vocational School for his assistance with data collection. I am also deeply appreciative to Dr. James A. Nolan, Director of the Behavioral Science Laboratory, Norfolk State University, Ms. Ruth Rose, teacher at Hunter College, City University of New York, and Dr. Alton Thompson, Professor of Sociology at the Agricultural and Technical State University, Greensboro, North Carolina, for editorial assistance and to Mr. Obie Smith, Mass Communications Department, Norfolk State University, for encouragement.

My special thanks are extended to Ms. Paula C. Briggs, Department of Mass Communications, Norfolk State University, for assisting data collection. And I am deeply appreciative to the 79 African-Amerian male dropouts, 238 African-American male seniors, and l66 white male seniors who made this study possible.

Annie S. Barnes

CONTENTS

LIST OF TABLES

List of Tables

List of Tables

List of Tables

PREFACE

The theme in this book is retention of African-American males in high school. Specifically, it is concerned with African-American male dropouts, African-American male stayins, and white male stayins in five high schools in Norfolk, Virginia. So far, almost everything that has been written about African-American male students in the public schools has focused on how to make schools effective, special programs implemented to enhance retention, curriculum needs, and racial inequality. Few ethnographic studies and related research focus on underlying reasons that explain why the collective African-American male drops out of high school and ways he experiences racism (inequality in school). Also, as far as I have been able to determine, school ethnographies do not compare successful males and dropouts to determine how to keep students from dropping out of school. Thus, there seems to be a very special need for a study of this type in the existing school ethnographies.[This study focuses on personal and structural problems experienced by African-American male high school dropouts and personal and structural factors that prevented the African-American male stayins and white high school male stayins from dropping out of school.] To help make this ethnography sound, the earlier ethnographies, speeches on education, and related research, from slavery until now, are used to inform this ethnography on retention of students in high school.

Therefore, Part I reviews relevant literature about the education of African-Americans from slavery until the present. Part II describes the methodologies of this study. In Part III the background characteristics of Norfolk, Virginia African-American male high school dropouts are analyzed to determine what insights they provide about leaving high school and related aspects of their behavior. Once the background of the African-American male dropouts was determined, emphasis was placed on personal reasons for dropping out of school. The dropouts explained their school problems, told why they dropped out of high school, and what could have been done to keep them from dropping out of high school. Also, Part III concerns structural factors in the school, criminal justice system, and family that caused the respondents to drop out of school. In Part IV emphasis is placed on African-American male stayins in the five Norfolk, Virginia High Schools and white high school male stayins in Norfolk. Their background, school traits, and future plans are described. PART V is comparative. It compares characteristics of the African-American male dropouts, African-American male stayins, and white male stayins; and determines a potential African-American male dropout. The concluding part, Part VI, concerns policy based on the findings in the three study populations.

PART I

INTRODUCTION

As noted in the Preface, this chapter discusses literature related to the education of African-American high school students and dropouts. For purposes of this study, a dropout is "any one whom we could determine interrupted his or her high school education at some point, including terminal dropouts, individuals who returned to school and obtained a high school diploma and those who obtained a GED" (Mensch and Kand 1988:98).

Educational Orientations

James Coleman and Thomas Hoffer provided two orientations of schooling. Accordingly, public schools"...have been designed to open broad horizons to the child" and as a major element in social mobility" (Coleman and Hoffer 1987:3). The second orientation is designed for private schools. Essentially, they are an extension of the family's values which make functional communities (Coleman and Hoffer 1987: 4, 6). Functional communities transmit the social structure of the adult community through private schools where the interactional level is high between the school and parents (Coleman and Hoffer 1987:6-7). Moreover, Coleman and Hoffer concluded that the verbal and math skills are higher in the private than public schools (1987:92). Public high schools need to pattern themselves after private schools and poor African-Americans will do just as well as whites. That is, public high schools must obtain highly prepared teachers with outstanding skills and knowledge and provide extra help through resources that are built into the school, and poor African-Americans will do just as well. In comparing public and private schools, it is also important to note the tutoring programs, comraderie between teachers and students, dedicated and highly qualified teachers, and the climate in college preparatory schools as compared to public school teachers who may leave school promptly at 2:30 P.M. or whenever the official school day ends.

Further, there are two other dominant schools of thought about education in the American society. One school is the Effective School Movement led by Ronald Edmonds. "In 1970, while serving as an Assistant Superintendent of Schools for the state of Michigan, Edmonds developed the concept of effective schools" (Comer et al. 1987-88:189). According to Comer et al., Edmonds defined effective schools as those which are "'sufficiently powerful to raise otherwise mediocre pupils to levels of instructional effectiveness they might not ordinarily have thought they could aspire to'" (1987-88: 189) Edmonds, according to Comer et al., also noted that five characteristics of an effective school are "Style of leadership, Instructional emphasis, Climate, Implied expectations derived from teacher, and Presence and use of and response to standardized instruments for increasing pupil progress" (1987-88: 190). Also, "Edmonds reasoned that the lack of achievement of some students is a political rather than a genetic issue in that the schooling of some students is not important to us as a nation" (Comer et al. 1987:190). Moody and Moody cited Edmonds and others who provide other elements for effective schools. Some of the elements are: "Principals who are instructional leaders, an effective learning philosophy, an effective climate or atmosphere, teacher expectations and process, and monitoring student progress" (Moody and Moody 1987-88: 177-184).

The second dominant school of thought about education is led by James Coleman and Christopher Jenks. According to Moody and Moody, "Studies by James Coleman and Christopher Jenks have led many educators to erroneously believe that schools cannot be effective for low socioeconomic (SES) urban black students; moreover, both Coleman and Jenks indicated that schools could not overcome the disadvantages implied by such low-income status" (1987:177).

The position taken in this book is that an effective public education can be achieved by inner city African-Americans and in fact, all African-Americans. An effective foursome: family, school, community, and criminal justice system can result in a top notch education for African-Americans on all social class levels. Poor African-Americans have the native ability to learn just as much as anyone else if effective teaching and a conducive climate are in place in schools. The underlying factor is that they must learn to learn while still infants and this process must be continued throughout their public school education. Learning to learn early is the key to success. The pattern will then be molded and African-Americans collectively will be among the highest achievers in the American society.

Since education is a high priority in the nation, effective schools should now become a reality. Lest we forget, effective schooling is not and has not been a reality in the lives of African-Americans,especially the male, who has not always had the opportunity to attend school a full school year at the time. The people who are criticizing his level of performance are the very ones who deprived him of an education to say nothing about an effective education, by requiring him to do farm labor, at an early age, for example. Rather than imprinting in mind that schools cannot do for African-Americans what they do for others, educational leaders should be showing what schools can do to make African-Americans anybody's educational equal. The call is for proud educators who educate all people.

African-Americans and Education: An Historical Review

To show the deep interest of African-Americans in learning and what whites as well as African-Americans can do to educate the so-called poor African-Americans, let us recall the beginning - the slavery era. According to Woodson "Many a sympathetic person taught slaves to read; in some cases, private teachers were bold enough to maintain Negro schools" (1922: 228). These schools were established in Savannah, Charleston, and Norfolk (Woodson 1922:228). Yet, slaves were not always privileged to formal education; instead, they learned from their occupations, from learned slaves, and from influential white men and children whom they accompanied to school, and servants learned from ministers and officials for whom they worked (Woodson 1919:206, 208). Even during slavery, there were whites deeply interested in African-Americans and who "... taught them regardless of public opinion and the law" (Woodson 1919:210).

Northern African-Americans educated contrabands; however, it appears that "the earliest school for contrabands was opened by Mary Chase, a free Negro of Alexandria, Virginia, on September 1, 1861. Two weeks later, Mrs. Mary Peake, an African-American woman, opened the first of the freedmen's aid societies schools, under the auspices of the American Missionary Association near Fortress Monroe, Virginia" (Meier and Rudwick 1966: 174).

Indeed, these individual efforts coupled with formal schools enabled some slaves and contrabands to read and write;for example,"The city Negroes of Virginia continued to maintain schools after the servile insurrection and state vigilance in executing laws" (Woodson 1919:217). Perhaps the most vivid case came to light in 1854. It occurred this way:

> In 1854 there was found in Norfolk, Virginia what the radically proslavery people considered a dangerous white woman. It was discovered that one Mrs. Douglass and her daughter had for three years been teaching a school maintained for educating Negroes (Woodson 1919:218).

She and her pupils were charged and acquitted with the understanding that Mrs. Douglass would not commit the same crime (Woodson 1919: 218).

Nevertheless, the missionaries and the War department worked together to educate African-Americans. For example, "... in 1863-4, in Louisiana, it was the military authorities who created the first system of public schools for freedmen in New Orleans and its environs" (Meier and Rudwick 1966:175). The War Department and the missionaries received large sums of money from the Freedmen's Bureau between 1866-1870 to educate African-Americans (Meier and Rudwick 1966:175).

It was in the early 1860s that formal education was made available to Southern African-Americans; and then it was usually provided for contra-

bands by freedmen and societies. Moreover, it was only a generation earlier that it first became a written law in the Northern states (Meier and
Rudwick 1966: 176).

This early educational system for African-Americans has strong implica-
tions for today. In the schools supported by missionary societies, the War
Department, and the Freedmen's Bureau, the "ex-slaves had a passion for
learning, Negroes of all ages and both sexes went to school, and African-
American children missed fewer days out of school than white children
(Meier and Rudwick 1966:176).

Even though Congress enfranchised African-Americans in 1867 and
there were reforms instituting public education, segregated schools did not
adequately educate the African-Americans (Meier and Rudwick 1966: 176-
177). Individuals recognized the inadequacy of segregated schools around
the middle of the nineteenth century.

Can it possible be that individuals approaching the twenty-first century
do not notice the inadequacies of currently segregated de facto and integrated public schools? I hardly think so. The vision seems clear; neither
school is meeting the needs of African-American males. Even if they are
learning to learn and learning in all African-American schools,they are not
learning to learn how to negotiate Black-white relationships, a prerequiste
for progress.

The missionaries in the nineteenth century correctly assessed the situation and assumed the burden of educating African-American ex-slaves.
The teachers of the time had goals they desired their students to achieve.
First of all, they wanted ex-slaves to be educated enough to function as
free men; then, they wanted them to achieve middle class status by empha-
sizing thrift, industry, and Christian character (Meier and Rudwick
1966:77). Indeed, if a century and a half ago whites and African-Americans
chose these as educational goals, these and many more goals should be the
baseline of education today.

After emancipation when African-Americans began to have greater opportunities, two African-American leaders charted what they considered to
be the right course of African-American education. They were Booker T.
Washington and W. E. B. DuBois. Like Woodson, both scholars agreed
that when African-Americans achieve education they should "... hand it
over to the greatest possible number of those who needed it" (Scott and
Stowe 1917: 17). However, Washington focused on industrial education
(1969: 9-29) and educating the masses (Scott and Stowe 1917: 17) while
Dubois was concerned first with educating the "Talented Tenth" (1969:33-
75). It was his idea to provide a college education for the most able and
send them out to pull the masses up; also, those who had lesser talents

could then go into vocational jobs as suggested by Washington (1969:33-
75). DuBois underscored his position when he said, "I insist that the object
of all true education is not to make men carpenters, it is to make carpenters
men" (1969:63). Yet he was an advocate of manual training and trade
teaching for Black young men (Dubois 1969: 62, 63). Further, he said,
"Education must not simply teach work-it must teach Life" (Dubois
1969:75). Dubois believed that the quickest way to raise the Negro in the
scale of civilization was to strengthen his character, increase his knowledge, and teach him to earn a living (1969:57).

Though DuBois and Washington differed in where the emphasis on education should be placed, both agreed that African-Americans need to be
educated. Washington came to be known as the leader of the Negro people. As a result, he made numerous speeches in which he talked about
how education could become the opportunity of the Negro. Interestingly,
he provided instructions that are still appropriate today.He encouraged
African-Americans to work together and whites to employ and train them
and discontinue destroying the confidence of African-Americans (Scott
and Stowe 1917:20). Moreover, he suggested to Blacks that they discontinue geographical mobility and become successful where they are
(Scott and Stowe 1917:20). He chided those who were indolent, shiftless,
unreliable, and vicious (Scott and Stowe 1917:20).

Washington spoke to another issue significant still. African-Americans
should live near whites in order to: "... have the benefit of them and in
those matters in which the older and stronger race excels" (Scott and
Stowe 1917:35). Not only yesterday, but today, African-Americans need to
break out of housing developments, other low rent housing neighborhoods, and enter middle class neighborhoods thus benefiting educationally
and socially by associating with whites who for generations have received
an education while African-Americans built the country with back breaking labor in fields, forests, factories, and labor intensive businesses.

Washington's encouragement for African-Americans to live near whites
is grounded in fact. African-Americans need to live near whites or use bus-
ing at every level of the school system to create integrated schools because, otherwise, they cannot learn informally what white youth have
learned from their parents; nor can they learn formally what white teachers
have learned over many more years of professional training. If African-
Americans remain academically isolated, they are likely to continue to lag
behind whites. For example, Reid stated that "In most of the states where
there are separate schools for Negroes,the schools for white children are
below the national average, yet Negro schools are only about half as well
supported as white schools" (1940: 39). Writing almost two decades
later,Ginzberg noted that "In the North and South, in segregated
schools,"the Negro receives inferior education" (1956:57).

I know there are two schools of thought in our country:(1) segregated schools and(2)integrated schools. Both are failing in their role to educate African-American males. The problem may be resolved by the development of higher quality public schools, including, of course, high schools geared to the needs of all children,recognizing any special needs of African-Americans. That is, African-American males should be prevented from dropping out of school.Ginzberg hinted at the dropout problem when he stated that African-American males achieve fewer years of schooling than whites (1956:60). The obvious question is Why? The answer is given in subsequent chapters.

However, at this point it should be noted that the United States Congress has shown interest in obtaining more schooling for all citizens.For example, Gibbs calls attention to congressional issues aimed at preventing school dropouts.Unless alternatives are employed, a high school dropout is at risk the remainder of his life. The 100th Congress recognized this and passed such bills as the School Dropout Demonstration Act of 1987, the School Dropout Retention and Recovery Act of 1987, and the School Dropout Demonstration Assistance Act of 1987 (Gibbs 1988: 326). Gibbs noted that "A significant feature of all of these bills is the promise of a variety of educational, psychological, and social support services for youth who are at high risk for failing or dropping out of school" (1988: 326). Who are the children at risk? All children are at risk, but when comparing African-American and white children,it is African-American children who are at greater risk.For example, on the national level in 1989, 4.5 percent of all high school students dropped out of school in grades 10-12 (U. S. Department of Commerce, 1990). Compared to the national percentage, Norfolk (Grades 9-12, i.e. high school) experienced an 8.7 percent dropout rate the first semester of the 1989-90 school term; African-American males contributed overwhelmingly to the Norfolk high school dropout rate, which was 6.2 percent of the Black high school population while the white male dropout rate was 3.1 percent (i.e. Norfolk Public School System, 1990) of the white students.

Early African-American scholars did not only bemoan the inferior education given to African-American children, but they did something about it or at least they tried. For example, Woodson described the correct way to educate African-Americans. First of all, he stated that "The large majority of the Negroes who have put on the finishing touches of our best colleges are all but worthless in the development of their people" (Woodson 1972:2). Hence, as Washington and DuBois, Woodson perceived "The seat of the trouble" as the need for educated African-Americans to develop the race; further, Woodson essentially calls for an"anti-lynching" campaign in African-American education (1972: 3-4). Woodson noted that someone had said, "...to handicap a student by teaching him that his black face is a curse and that his struggle to change his condition is hopeless is the worst sort of lynching. It kills one's aspiration and dooms him to vagabondage and crime" (Woodson 1972.3). In Woodson's language: Are the educational professionals in the 1990s lynching African-Americans, especially males, in the school? Has physical lynching been replaced by intellectual and psychological lynching by failure to maintain African-American males in high school?

Woodson added another insight.That is, according to him, classroom lynching of African-Americans accounts for some of the laziness and crime among young African-American males (1972:8).Thus, the behavior whites accuse African-Americans of becomes a self-fulfilling prophecy when they experience classroom and principal-office lynchings at the hands of African-Americans as well as white educators.Interestingly, Woodson focused on intra-race lynching that results from lynching techniques learned from whites (Woodson 1972:8). Woodson seems to have put to rest the notion that all Black or African-American schools are the answer. He suggested that African-American children can be lynched in their own as well as in integrated schools. The question to be raised in the 1990s is whether there is educational lynching of African-American males? Is there lack of opportunity for African-American male students to compete and negotitate successfully with whites as life must dictate in future years. Are they learning to learn the processes of achievement and implementing them in the school setting? Are there ineffective counseling, teaching, disciplining, and caring? These are the tools that lynch African-American children and result in a relatively high drop out rate. The lynch mobs can be white or African-American.Wherever they are found, they need to be eliminated.

Woodson gave directions for African-Americans who teach their people. He admonished them to present correctly the differences between the races and put African-American history in every level of the curriculum and enable students to excel in higher education (Woodson 1972:8, 14, 21). Dent has noted that "The lack of emphasis on African and African-American culture, history and achievement in the school curriculum undermines the progress of Black children" (1989:58). Woodson raised a significant question: Why don't teachers in segregated schools change the curriculum and "uplift Negroes"? He concluded that Negro teachers were powerless under segregation; furthermore, Woodson stated that "Even with Negroes in charge, it is doubtful that things will change" (Woodson 1972: 22, 23).This all came about, he says,by whites shaping the minds of African-Americans the way they would have them function; besides in Woodson's thinking, the African-American leader is without a vision for his/her people (Woodson 1972:23).

According to Woodson, these so-called miseducated African-American leaders defend the system of miseducation of African-Americans because this is their living; when a few miseducated African-Americans act otherwise, they are crushed by Caucasins (Woodson 1972:24). As far as Woodson was concerned, "miseducated Negroes are of no service to themselves and none to the white man" (Woodson 1972: 24). In other words, miseducated African-Americans don't put in place a good education for their people and technology can do the white man's menial tasks.

African-Americans and Education: Current Issues

As a result of all these circumstances Woodson brought to the surface, the struggle for education of African-Americans continues. It is even more pronounced among African-American males. However, first it must be understood that "... many individual Black males have, notwithstanding the present public education system, negotiated the public elementary and secondary school system with success and furthered their life long development" (Patton 1981: 211).The concern here is mainly with the collective African-American male who makes up the masses."The collective African-American male is the most oppressed group affected by the educational system" (Patton 1981:212). What this means, on the basis of empirical and statistical evidence, is that "... the educational system has been mentally,emotionally, and physically as well as spiritually brutal and oppressive toward the collective Black male" (Patton 1981: 212).

The important question is: What can be done to help all African-Americans males, thereby benefiting the collective African-American male? Patton suggests that the Black experience and the Black traditional culture be incorporated into the American system of education (1981:212). Also, Holland noted that "A crying need in all education not merely Negro education is a revision of teaching materials to reflect the fact that Negroes exist: that they have played a part in building America from colonial days until the present and have contributed to every aspect of American cultural,social, economic, political, and scientific life" (1969:225). That is, "integrate the Negro into the language arts and social science curriculum of American schools..." (Holland 1969:225). Along with this change, Patton recommends that "...American education must define Black strengths and weaknesses and respond to these realities in ways consistent with the nation's collective essence" (Patton 1981:212).For example, if African-Americans have a problem speaking and writing standard English and doing mathematical calculations and reasoning, teach to the problem and reserve Shakespeare until the prerequisites have been adequately taught and learned.

There are other ways the American school system can improve the education of the collective African-American male and all African-Americans. Holland suggested improving the educational system by putting the best teachers in a school district into blighted areas, that is, poor black schools, and replacing catastrophic guidance counseling with motivating counseling that helps American youth (1969: 208, 212, 222, 225, 228, 229). In effect, this would enable the collective African-American male to be the educational equal of the collective white male; and the achievers of both races to be educational equals. There does not seem to be anything wrong with the races being equal educationally. In fact, it seems advantageous for the nation. Let the schools be among the first to relinquish racism--inequality--and make the collective African-American male as educated as any student in America.

In schools, administrators have the primary responsibility in establishing rules and implementing them fairly across the races. It has been said that "Schools must help students to focus on common goals rather than wallow in racial conflicts" (The Lindseys 1974: 1855). In one study Bachman and Van Diernen, asked young males to name the most important national problems; "Racial tensions were mentioned second most often among major national problems" (Bachman and Van Diernen 1962: 35). Dent verifies this finding. For example, some white males still call African-American males "Nigger." In one particular case, as told by Dent, a white male yelled "Nigger" to an African-American young male during gym.The African-American male didn't know what it meant, but judging by the white male's eyes it was not the right thing to say.Later,on different days, the African-American male followed the name calling with a push, a punch, and a report to the teacher. The teacher merely told them to play fair. So it continued and the African-American male beat the white boy. That got the teacher's attention.The teacher grabbed the African-American male, carried him to the office and paddled him. The African-American male was only six years old at the time; now he is seventeen and his eyes flash with anger when he remembers the incident (Dent 1989:56).Dent also noted that a sixteen year old student in New Jersey told him that when there is a fight at school between the races, the administration always approaches the African-American student, believes he started it, and "...come down harder on Black kids than on white ones" (1989:57).Even with all the problems the African-American male student faces, "The Best Way Out of the Ghetto is to spend time studying science and math after school and not practicing his skyhook" (Fisher 1978: 240).

Nevertheless, "Students must be made to realize that school is for everyone, that intimidation is not a part of the curriculum and will not be tolerated" (The Lindseys 1974: 185).To make this a reality, "Office personnel staff needs race relations seminars" (The Lindseys 1974: 204-205). The principal is the key person in the school offices. He can make a difference; for example, it is up to him to see that all students have the same privileges and are held equally accountable for their actions when they run counter to (those) privileges (The Lindseys 1974: 206).

"The low-level adaptive mechanism of racism is a result of anxiety and fear and affects all of us" (Comer 1989:360). In writing about racism in the education of young children, Comer suggested that teachers be given pre-and in-service work shops to learn how their behavior impacts the learning of African-American children; they should be trained to address the needs of minority children and contribute to their development."Angry alienated youth is a result and affects all of us" (Comer 1972: 227). Probably this alienation contributes to their violence. Hence, Strickland noted that "60 young Black men compared with every 10 young white men will more likely die violent, often self-inflicted deaths;" in other words, "Homicide and suicide kill more of our 15 to 24 year-olds than any other means" (1989:51). Perhaps, in part, this behavior results from alienation.

There is evidence that African-Americans are alienated by the schools. For example, Wolfstetter-Kausch and Gaier in a study of 32 females and 26 males in the black lower class, found alienation from both society and school to be pervasive (1981:471). Consequently, counseling for African-American students should be concerned with personality development with emphasis on the "child's physical, social, emotional, and moral development as well as his learning process (Holland 1969: 228). Lee has identified the functions of the counselor of African-American children. He found that Personal social growth (Facilitating the development of positive Black self-identity and Facilitating the development of positive interpersonal relations and responsible behavior); Academic Achievement (Facilitating the development of positive attitudes toward academic achievement and facilitating the development of academic skills and competencies); and Career Development (Facilitating the vocational choice and career development process) are functions of the counselor (Lee 1982:96). Moreover, Lee stated that the counselor of African-American children who experience "systemic insensitivity" should account for the problem and alleviate it; in other words, determine whether the problems are in the educational system or in the children (1982:98).Additionally, the counselor of African-American children "can serve as an important link between the home, the larger Black community, and the school" (Lee 1982:99). Counselors are also "trouble shooters" before the students' "problems" get out of hand (The Lindseys 1974:175). Moreover, counselors can provide new ways of thinking about a problem, stand between a wrong and right student-made decision, and serve as a friend in court so-to-speak" (Lindseys 1974: 176).

If the color of the student makes a difference or racial chauvinism exists, counselors need race relations courses (The Lindseys 1974: 176).Perhaps they should enroll in race relations courses taught by African-American teachers with the Afro-centric perspective. This is important because "... experience has shown that prejudice and stereotyping can even be found in the office of the counselor" (The Lindseys 1974: 174). For instance, counselors may encourage students to follow vocations when the students desire and are capable of becoming professionals, such as a dentist (The

Lindseys 1974: 174). "Racism is a dead-end street, leading only to frustra-
tion, fear, hatred of others, and finally to a chilling, dehumanizing self-ha-
tred" (The Lindseys 1974: 210).

Teachers of African-Americans can also make their struggle less difficult
and their success rate higher.It seems to be a simple matter to achieve;the
teacher needs to be excellent and fair, use the word "some students" rather
than "all students" and share with every child "... their own sense of inner
security, their own zest for what they are doing, and their own interest in
the fates of their students" (The Lindseys 1974: 156, 159, 167). Rosenthal
and Jacobson concluded on the basis of a control and experimental group
that in the latter the teacher's expectations were high; she demonstrated
this in her facial expressions, postures, and perhaps touch and possible
changes in teaching techniques" (1968:180). These behaviors "...may have
helped the child learn by changing his self concept, his expectations of his
own behavior, and his motivation, as well as his cognitive style and skills"
(Rosenthal and Jacobson 1968: 180). Using Rosenthal and Jacobson as a
model Good also found that some teachers vary their behavior between
low and high achievers (1981:416). The twelve findings indicate differences
in seating, attention, calling on students, waiting for answers, criticism, and
praise (Good 1981: 416). The African-American student does not need to be
subjected to differential treatment; instead, he needs teachers who understand and enhance his self concept.

Mack (1987: 25) identifies thirteen ways to enhance the self concept of
African-American school children (1987: 25).Thus, "Urban schools that
teach poor children successfully have strong leadership and a climate of
expectation that students will learn" (Edmonds 1979:15). This positive influence will reap results. On the other hand, " the negative attitude of a
teacher toward students has an adverse effect upon the student's achievement"(Johnson 1974:1).According to Johnson, "Unqualified teachers have
frequently relied upon fear as the means of enforcing discipline, and the
Negro teachers in the rural South are no exception. Poorly trained teachers
often try to conceal their ignorance and to terrify the pupils" (Johnson
1967:122).   This kind of teacher makes children dread the opening of
school (Johnson 1967: 122). Kenneth Clark indicates that Black students
simply are not being taught; as a result they fail (1965:128). Dent noted
that "Many educators believe that negative stereotypes of Black men-as
lazy, violent troublemakers-are locked into the psyche of the educational
system, and that these images influence teachers when they teach Black
boys and explain why these children fail in school" (1989: 56).In other
words, "What we need in our schools are secure and mature men and
women who have feelings for their students and who respect them as well
as empathize with their problems, who like the subjects they teach, who
are both good talkers and good listeners" (Foster 1986: 290). Moreover, it
is suggested that "There is a higher degree of socialization and teacher-

child interaction where the classroom is defined as an efficient workroom and where the child's play is viewed as work" (Morgan 198:50)."This notion of changing school climate is consistent with the research on school effectiveness that found that schoolwide changes are needed to improve students' academic success, but it in no way compromise the emphasis on high academic expectations for black students" (Gilbert II and Gay 1985: 134).   Such outstanding teachers recognize that the outside world of African-Americans is brought into the school. Foster stated "I have witnessed some outstanding teacher--student relationships grow from violent encounters between tough male streetcorner students and tough male teachers" (1986: 290).

Choosing substitute teachers is another important factor in helping African-Americans to graduate from high school. This means that "The substitute teacher should never think of his job as merely a "substitute for the real thing," but as a much needed helper on the road of education for our young (The Lindseys 1974: 176).

Perhaps Proctor best sums up the model teacher who should be in charge of all African-American students, especially males. He stated that "We must indeed assure children that each of them is somebody. We must provide them with teachers who believe that they can achieve. We must encourage support from parents and other community members" (1978: 200S).

Special School Programs to Enhance Retention

African-American male high school students have received some attention and some plans for enhancing their education have been put in place in a few cities across America. Because "of the poor quality of education their children were receiving in the established school system, the idea of: black teachers teaching only black students has risen" (The Lindseys 1974: 152).   The response to this notion is there are "Many dedicated white teachers who are anxious to do, and have done, a good job in teaching black as well as white students (Lindseys 1974: 152). A related plan for African-American males has been decided for Milwaukee, Wisconsin. Thus, "The school board has voted to create two "African-American immersion schools" in a pilot program that seeks to emphasize black culture, build self-esteem, and promote the rewards of responsible behavior (The Virginian-Pilot and the The Ledger Star, September 30, 1990). This would separate African-American males from other males and all females in an experiment to improve their educational status. A group of African-American parents has carried the proposal beyond the creation of two schools for African-American males. A group of parents in Milwaukee announced its intention to obtain legislation to create an independent district or a special neighborhood district within the city school system; and it would be 97 percent African-American (Bell 1987-88: 136).The separatists desire parental involvement, teacher morale, and accountability to students; perhaps more importantly their plan calls for mastery of basic skills, development of analytical ability needed for effective functioning in today's world and their confidence to influence, control, and change the world that come from knowledge of the values and strength of Black history and culture (Bell 1987-88: 137).

It has also been suggested that African-American male classes may curb the African-American male dropout rate. According to William Saunders, Executive Director, National Alliance of Black School Educators, "We ought to look at the way we are training these young men...If it means training them separately, fine" (Lyons 1990:10). The high suspension and expulsion rates have caused educators to seek these alternative means of educating the African-American male. For example, Garibaldi and Bartley reported on pushouts and dropouts. On the basis of the Children's Defense Fund (CDF) survey (1972-73),they cite,"Non-white students comprised only 38 percent of the total enrollment in this survey but accounted for 43% of the expulsions, 49% of the suspensions (black students accounted for 47% of the total), and more than half of the 3 1/2 million days lost by suspension. Moreover, non-white students were suspended for an average of 4.3 days per suspension, compared to 3.5 days for white students"(1990:228). Similarly, in Milwaukee, "Black males accounted for 50% of all suspensions last year, although they represent less than 28 % of the enrollment" (The Virginian Pilot and The Ledger-Star 1990:19).

Garibaldi and Bartley suggest alternatives to suspensions and expulsions. They suggest that in-school suspensions include: (1) time-out rooms for short-term referrals such as a class period; (2) in-school suspension centers,designed as full-day alternative programs located on the school campus, where "master teachers" could assist students with the daily classwork assigned by their regular teachers; and (3) counseling/ guidance centers where students were required to meet on a regular basis with a counselor during or after the school day to discuss infractions" (Garibaldi and Bartley 1990: 228-229). Robinson, an educator,stated,"But in all fairness, ... teachers should be provided with adequate training to deal more effectively with students who may be deviant or just of a different race or culture" (Wiley III 1990:17).

The Ohio County schools reduced dropout rates through communicating with the families. Their sequential plan of intervention included five stages: (1) exit interviews were conducted with students who left school prior to graduation (2) the home visitor, counselors, administrators, and teachers gave the names of potential dropouts to the home-school visitor, (3) a dropout reentry program was created, and (4) using data from a study established a "profile of the junior high and elementary student for whom early intervention in a dysfunctional life-style was paramount" (Marockie and Jones 1987: 200-202). The fifth stage of the intervention process was called "Care Call"; a "Care-Call was made daily to each student whose name appeared on the absence list..."; some of the callers were retired teaching professionals (Marockie and Jones 1987: 201). It was concluded that "...techniques as simple as daily phone calls, visits in the home, and personal contacts are still the most effective way to communicate" (Marockie and Jones 1987:204).

Another home-school prevention project was called I Promise. The state superintendent in West Virginia launched the program. I Promise ads were placed in the newspapers asking students "to learn more, to work harder, and to plan for their future " (Truby 1987:210); "When parents or students signed the pledge and sent it in, they sent them a laminated pocket copy of the pledge so that they could carry it in their wallet or pocketbooks" (Truby 1987:211). The spinoff from the program was positive (Truby 1987: 211).

Still another school dropout prevention program was developed in Pittsburgh. It focuses on the community and schools working together. In Pittsburgh, "Their overall cumulative dropout rate is 27 percent" (Monaco and Parr 1988:39). The remainder of the characteristics of many African-American and white students caused them to be described as a disadvantaged culture (Monaco and Parr 1988:39). Pittsburgh organized six types of vocational schools: Vocational and technical courses, Occupational and Academic Skills for the Employment of Students, The Select Employment Trainee Program, a high-tech magnet school, a vocational education magnet school, and a school within a school (Monaco and Parr 1988: 40). Concerning the latter, which is housed in the Westinghouse High School, visitors from as far away as Indonesia have observed its Business and Finance Academy (Monaco and Parr 1988: 40).Alice Carter, director of education at Pittsburgh's Urban League said:

> I've been trying for 20 years to make the system work for minorities. The concern led me to devise a dropout prevention program based on a controversial premise:that if you take certain students who aren't doing well in school, persuade them that they have talent and can learn skills, make them feel special, and give them incentives to learn,they will turn their lives around.

> And doggone if they haven't. One female student in our program's first graduating class, for example,came into the program as leader of a school gang. She left the duly elected president of the whole high school's senior class. (Monaco and Parr 1988:40).

Carter noted that the banks were accustomed to the "Adopt a School" plan but not to making real changes, "such as developing a finance-oriented curriculum (Monaco and Parr 1988: 41). The Westinghouse program does not include hard-core troublemakers, like drug abusers and sex offenders (Monaco and Parr: 41). Carter and others convinced the five area banks to sponsor the project and received donations from other sources (Monaco and Parr:41). In general, vocational schools have been established in Pittsburgh to prevent the high risk students, especially minorities, from dropping out of high school. Moreover, the students obtained jobs in the sponsoring banks and other industries. Yet, in 1987 Pittsburgh was not satisifed with its schools' holding power. To help remedy the situation, in 1987, the Annie E. Casey Foundation asked Pittsburgh to prepare a proposal for a five year program to implement "a New Futures Initiative, which is a school-community partnership that boosts academic achievement and youth employment and curtails youth dropout and pregnancy rates" (Monaco and Parr 1988:41). "The Casey grant gives the city an unprecedented opportunity to expand the city's focus on the needs of its at-risk youth." (Monaco and Parr 1988:41).

Similarly, in Chicago, 43 percent of the entering freshmen drop out of high school before graduating. They found in this city that "students who have goals and students enrolled in career-vocational programs are less likely to drop out than those in traditional school programs" (Azcoitia and Viso 1987:33). The Chicago Public Schools with help from the State Office of Vocational and Technical Education, have created a vocational support services team for disadvantaged, handicapped, and limited English proficient youth (Azcoitia and Viso 1987:33). As part of the vocational support services team, Chicago has The Student Services Corporation. It "...provides tutoring services to vocational students. The tutors--disadvantaged students themselves--are selected, trained, and supervised by a teacher, and are paid for their services" (Azcoitia and Viso 1987:33). The program is considered successful (Azcoitia and Viso 1987: 33).

In 1987, Memphis initiated the Inner-City Schools Improvement Project (Herenton 1987:209).This program "...combines the elements of the Effective Schools Movement with the strategies of a holistic community-based intervention/prevention approach" (Herenton 1987:210). The program also views urban education in the context of "community schools;" the community includes the students and their families, neighbors, and friends (Herenton 1987: 210). Besides, the Inner-City Schools Improvement Project also acknowledges the responsibilities of social service, welfare, and health care systems, churches, civic organizations, businesses, government agencies, and the criminal justice system (Herenton 1987:210). Further, the Project views the community as a resource to be tapped and as a point of intervention and prevention (Herenton 1987: 210). The program appears geared to elementary school children and focuses on parental education, tutoring and education outside the regular classes, non-tuition remedial summer school programs, peers, substance abuse, pregnancy, role models, computer education, an African-American library and research center, and work with social welfare, human,and medical services (Herenton 1987: 210-215). They added a System-Wide Achievement Team (SWAT) to improve the instructional leadership in the seven targeted schools, increase the academic focus in the school, improve the schools' climate, raise expectations of teachers,students, and parents, and provide continuing assessment of student performance (Herenton 1987: 215). The Inner-City Schools Improvement Project was developed because of "unemployment and underemployment, generational welfarism, poor academic achievement, high absenteeism, suspension and dropout rates, a rising incidence of teenage pregnancy, drug and alcohol abuse, crime and delinquency, and lack of access to community resources (Herenton 1987: 209).

The Chesapeake, Virginia School System has a program called Student and Faculty Exchange (SAFE) in its Western Branch High School. It does not involve any money; "this program is funded by the enthusiasm of 100 teacher volunteers" (O'Keefe 1990: D4). The program targets at risk students between grades 9 and 12. The concern is with students who are behind their peers one or more years, show a history of absenteeism, disruptive classroom behavior, and membership in a family of low socioeconomic standing (O'Keefe 1990: D4). Before participating in the program, parents must give their permission; "Less than one percent has refused" (O'Keefe 1990: D4). The program is successful, the dropout rate at Western Branch High School is 3.7, the rate for the city of Chesapeake is 3.9 percent, and the state figure is 4.7 percent (O'Keefe 1990: D4+).

In regard to Virginia, the Governor, Douglas L. Wilder, asked the students in Virginia to write him letters informing him how to keep them in school. Six major ways suggested were:

Make classes more stimulating and teachers less boring.

During classes,play soft music laced with subliminal messages about good grades.

Put nurseries into schools for student-mothers.

Reward students who do well with cash or discount coupons that will get them into concerts or movies at lower prices.

Force fast-food restaurants to hire only workers who can show a high school diploma so that dropouts don't have an easy alternative.

Tell parents they have to help children with their homework and show that school is important (Armao 1990:D5).

Indeed, parents should be an essential part of their children's education. They have an important job to do; for example, "Minority parents must begin to direct more attention to the intellectual capabilities of their sons and daughters" (Hale 1978:205S). Why? According to Kenneth Clark, "A key component of the deprivation which afflicts ghetto children is that generally their teachers do not expect them to learn. This is certainly one possible interpretation of the fact that ghetto children in Harlem decline in relative performance and in I. Q. the longer they are in school" (1965:132).Therefore,it is not fair for parents to leave the fate of their children to teachers, counselors, and administrators. Also, they should get to know their children's teachers, counselors, school secretaries, and administrative staff. It has been reported that "On many occasions black students, parents, and visitors have remarked on the coolness or rudeness displaced to them by office personnel-both white and black" (The Lindseys 1974: 206). In fact, "It is unrealistic to expect parents to become involved in an institution that treats them and their children without respect" (1978: 208S).

Current Research on Students

Turning to the student, certainly there are African-American students who present problems in school. Yet, most of them are not disruptive and incorrigible; "they have dreams and hopes of bettering themselves through education" (The Lindseys 1974: 145). The behavior of African-American males is not a one sided event. African-American males have been harassed in school. The result is that "In some student harassment school situations, principals and staff will be confronted with the fact that some black students engage in bullying and harassing behavior toward white students, and exhibit disrespect for teachers" (The Lindseys 1974:206-207). In such cases, teachers and administrative staff should resolve the problem immediately (The Lindseys 1974: 207).

When children experience rejection from teachers and other important adults, "The child fights back or seeks attention in the only way he or she knows how-through physical and verbal abuse..." (Comer 1972:224). It seems imperative that juvenile delinquents be kept in school. There is support for this perspective. Dunham and Alpert tested an empirically based prediction model of school dropout on a sample of 137 juvenile delinquents; some had dropped out while others were still students (1987: 45). They found the factors that predict if a juvenile delinquent will dropout of school. They are "...misbehavior in school, disliking school, the negative influence of peers with respect to dropping out and getting into trouble, and a marginal or weak relationship with parents" (Dunham and Alpert 1987:45). Because it is possible to predict whether delinquents will drop out of school, the home, school, and community need to have in place a plan to keep the delinquent in school. Of course juvenile delinquents aren't the only ones who drop out of school. "Some experts say teachers don't challenge Black male students, that school disciplinary policies are pushing boys out of the system, and that schools need to develop Afro-centric environments for Black children. Others talk of the need to combat student-group attitudes that nay say school" (Dunham and Alpert 1989:14).

Implications of Current Research and Programs

An attempt has been made to provide a comprehensive view of the African-American educational experience with emphasis on the male. Some progress has been made in improving his conditions; yet, a great deal more needs to be done to keep the African-American male in high school, help him obtain a sound education, graduate, and go to college. Hence, the bottom line is that something else needs to be done for the African-American male in the public school system even before he gets to elementary school.

Moreover, African-Americans need to do something for themselves. Srickland suggested that we return to the pre-Civil War practice of holding Negro Conventions (Scott and Stowe 1917:20). "But instead of meeting downtown, we should do so where the people are with whom we need to be in dialogue: in the streets, prisons, churches, schools, and so on" (1989:114). Further, Strickland admonishes African-Americans to find out what's going on in their own race and in the white race--essential knowledge for setting an agenda to improve the future of African-American men and women (1989:114).

This review of African-American education has shown it from its inception to its current status. There are many interesting points in the literature; for example, the Southern schools began with a segregated student populous and in 1992, more than a hundred years later, it is moving rapidly toward the same status. Also, the literature is vivid in its description of ways to make counselors, teachers, and administrators effective. An effective staff will do much to develop effective schools. The literature also takes into account racial inequality in the schools and the needs of low income students; yet, it also includes school problems that students bring from the streets to the classroom. Nevertheless, it is America's responsibility to make the schools effective.

PART II RESEARCH DESIGN

The Settings

The Five Norfolk High Schools

The study of the African-American male stayins and the white male stayins was conducted with seniors in the five Norfolk, Virginia High Schools: Granby, Lake Taylor, Norview, Maury, and Booker T. Washington (see Figure 1). A brief history of each school is presented to set the tone and establish the settings.

Granby High School. Granby Street High School, now officially Granby High School, is located in Talbot Park, on the West side of Granby Street in the Northwestern section of Norfolk. Both the street and the school are named after Mr. John Manner, Marquis of Granby, a hero of the Seven Years War. The twenty-four acre tract on which Granby was built was donated to the city of Norfolk by Mr. Minton W. Talbot. This land is part of what was once the historic Talbot Plantation which extended northward from the Granby Street Bridge.

The school first opened September, 1939 with Mr. Lemuel E. Games as principal and Mr. E. L. Lamberth as assistant principal. They were faced with the task of welcoming and orienting 1200 new and confused students, who were easily accomodated in the school then having a capacity of 1500. Dr. Theodore Smith the current principal, and his staff assisted the stayin and documentary studies at Granby High School.

Lake Taylor Senior High School. Lake Taylor High School is unique in design and function. It looms on the horizon near the eastern limits of the City of Norfolk, a multi-storied building, located on spacious grounds adjacent to placid Lake Taylor. It is the hub of an educational complex that includes a junior high school, an academy, and a four year college. Travelers on the Interstate Highway 64 that borders the eastern limits of the grounds take with them a panoramic view of one of the nation's newest and most imposing senior high schools--a five-million-dollar edifice.

Lake Taylor Senior High School opened its doors to students for the first time on Tuesday, September 5, 1967. The school accomodates students from grades nine through twelve.

Everything about the building and the educational program it houses reflects freedom at Lake Taylor Senior High School--freedom for teachers to teach and inspire and freedom for students to learn and develop responsibility. A city that makes such a big investment in the education of its youth is destined to be a great city! Mr. Raleigh Baggett, the current prin-

NORFOLK, VIRGINIA HIGH SCHOOLS

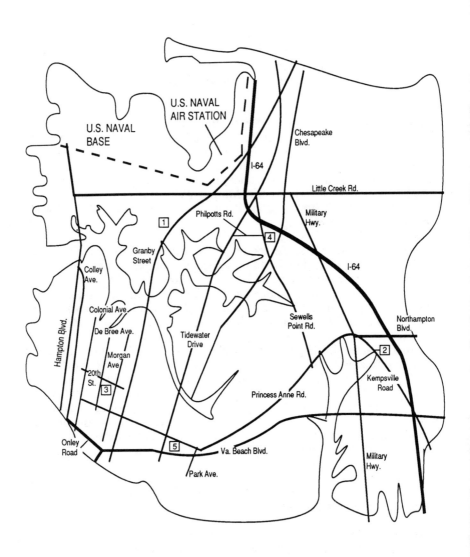

FIGURE 1

LEGEND

1. Granby High School
2. Lake Taylor High School
3. Maury High School

4. Norview High School
5. Booker T. Washington High School

cipal, and his staff made a significant contribution to the stayin and documentary research.

Maury High School. Built in 1910, Maury High School was the city's first high school and the second in the Southern Association of Colleges and Schools (SACS) accrediting body. Its graduates have held leadership positions in the city, state, and nation for eighty years. Situated in the Southwestern section of Norfolk in the historic downtown area, it is one-half mile from the Chrysler Museum and Center Theatre, home of the Virginia Opera Association, and two miles from both Norfolk State University and Old Dominion University. The proximity to these cultural and educational institutions has enriched Maury by the opportunities afforded the students and by the students themselves whose parents comprise some of their staff.

In 1970, the school began planning for an innovative modular scheduling, phase-elective program. Implemented in 1972, this nontraditional program was intended to meet the diverse needs of an integrated, urban high school. The staff at Maury designed and wrote the curriculum for all the courses; these nine-week phase electives ultimately became the basis for the citywide curriculum in English and later for the semester courses. This was an historic milestone in that it established Maury as a forerunner where change was concerned. The physical plant combines the best of the old traditional architecture with the modern amenities and technological sophistication. Mr. James Slaughter is the current principal of Maury and assisted both phases of our research.

Norview High School. In 1921, the first school building to go by the name of Norview was originally a farmhouse. Then in 1922, Norview students and their first principal, H. C. Barnes, moved into the new high school, what is now known as Norview Middle School.

In June 1953, the first cornerstone of the building now known as Norview High School was laid. In September 1954 the project was completed, and in 1955 the first students graduated from the new Norview High School situated in the Northeastern section of Norfolk.

Originally built to house 1400 students, Norview High's community of Norview was a part of Norfolk County, not the city of Norfolk. It is for this reason that Norview is the only high school in Norfolk that has a football field--it was built by Norfolk County. In 1955, Norview, along with the rest of Norfolk County, was annexed to the City of Norfolk.

The "new" Norview, a setting for this study, has seen only two principals. Mr. C. W. "Bolo" Perdue, who helped coach Norview's football teams in the late 1940s, had been the first principal until 1982, when he resigned and Mr. Claude Sawyer who assisted this research became principal.

The school mascot, the "Pilot" plane, usually a biplane, has an interesting origin. One of the early principals enjoyed amateur flying and often practiced in a field near Norview. Norview "Pilots" became the accepted mascot and the most unique, as one is unlikely to find another school's mascot to be the "Pilots" in the country.

Booker T. Washington High School. The history of Booker T. Washington High School dates back to April, 1911, when the Norfolk School Board agreed to endorse one year of high school education in connection with the elementary school at John T. West School for Negroes. In 1912, a second year was added and, in 1913, a third year was included. In May of 1914, the State Board of Education endorsed the high school and the local School board passed an act which gave Virginia its first accredited public high school for Negroes.

The following year saw such rapid growth that the board was forced to move the high school to a site on Princess Anne road. This site was offically occupied in 1917 and the school immediately changed its name to Booker T. Washington High School. In 1924, keeping pace with its own rapid growth, a new and then modern Booker T. Washington High School opened on Virginia Beach Boulevard, in the southern section of Norfolk, with a student body of 1750 in grades 7-12 and a faculty of 63 teachers.

During the 1920s and 1930s, under the leadership of Mr. Winston Douglas, Booker T. Washington High School rose to new heights of glory, earning the names "the Mighty Booker T" and "the Fighting Bookers." In 1961, Mr. Albert Preston took the helm and guided Booker T. Washington High School through many major social, economic, and educational changes with unaltered determination and quiet dignity.

In September of 1974, a new era began for Booker T. Washington High School. A modern eight million dollar school plant was opened. The formal dedication took place on Sunday, February 9, 1975. With its usual pride and determination,the student body and faculty look forward to carrying on the outstanding job that has been done over the past fifty years by Booker T. Washington High School in serving the community, the state, and the nation. Dr. Thomas A. Newby, the current principal and his counseling staff made an important contribution to the stayin and documentary studies.

Today, these five high schools educate all the races and ethnic groups in Norfolk, including whites, African-Americans, native Americans, and Asians. Moreover, the City of Norfolk takes pride in its schools by keeping them attractive and in good condition. Therefore, the setting for this study is comprised of monumental structures loved by the people of Norfolk, Virginia.

Housing Developments and Low Rent Housing Areas

Approximately all the African-American males in this study who dropped out of the five Norfolk, Virginia High Schools lived either in housing developments or other low rent housing areas. Of the 105 respondents, eleven lived in middle class neigborhoods while ninety four respondents lived in brick cinder block buildings with concrete floors or housing that was in need of repair. Therefore, the dropout segment of this study is about African-American males in poor families. As suggested in the concluding chapter in this book, special attention should be given to housing developments in American cities. Perhaps if dropping out of school is alleviated in housing developments, private low rent housing residents will also reap the benefits.

The Dropouts

The results reported in this book comprise a study on student retention in the ninth through twelfth grades in the five Norfolk, Virginia high schools. The research project was conducted in three stages. The first stage was initiated by Dr. Jesse Lewis, Vice President for Academic Affairs at Norfolk State University, who desired an understanding of why African-American males drop out of high school which curtails the African-American male college population. Paula Clark Briggs, a teacher in the Mass Communications Department at Norfolk State University, and I were immediately interested in the proposed project. The result was that I did a preliminary review of the literature, wrote the proposal, and constructed the interview schedule. Upon approval of the proposal by the Norfolk State University Research Committee and receipt of funding, the program was proceeded. A critical aspect of funding was the approval of a $10.00 check for each African-American male dropout who participated in the ethnography of African-American male dropouts.

Subsequently, I wrote a letter to the Superintendent of the Norfolk, Virginia Public School System and stated our desire to study the African-American males who dropped out of the five Norfolk High Schools during the first semester of the 1989-90 school term. Dr. Gene Carter, the superintendent, responded favorably and directed me to contact Dr. Anna Dodson, the Director of the Norfolk Public Schools Department of Research, Testing and Statistics. A copy of the proposed interview schedule was sent to her along with a request to conduct the study. The director agreed to the study and interview schedule and referred us to Mr. James Staton, the Supervisor of Student Affairs in the Norfolk Public School System, who is a high school dropout specialist and graduate of Norfolk

State University.The supervisor provided a printout in January, 1990 of the students who had dropped out of high school the first semester of the 1989-90 term.   The printout included the race, sex, birthdate, grade in which the student dropped out, home telephone number, if available, and address. In February, 1990, Briggs and I began contacting the dropouts for interviews. For students who had telephones, we interviewed them on the telephone while former students who did not have a telephone were inter- viewed in person. This was an arduous process. We crisscrossed the City of Norfolk countless times trying to locate the dropouts or find them at home.   Each interview lasted an average of one hour. Briggs collected ap- proximately one third of the interviews and I conducted the remainder. With few exceptions, the former students were very interested in respond- ing to the interview questions and some told us that we need not pay them. However, we explained that a $10.00 check per interview was part of the project and they accepted it. Others were pleased to receive $10.00 for their contribution.   However, the over-riding feature of the research process is that the dropouts had something to say and wanted to say it; moreover, dropping out was a traumatic experience--one they wished had never happened. And this was their opportunity to say so. Hence, we learned early, that dropping out of high school is a negative experience for the African-American males in our study.

Because a majority of the respondents were highly verbal, shortly after we began administering the interview schedule, additional information proved that we needed to add some in-depth questions; most of which we had not anticipated. They focused on quick temper, fighting in and out of school, sale of drugs, classroom procedures, racism in the classrooms, halls, and offices, administrative treatment, and the role of religion in their lives. Because these issues surfaced immediately, they were asked to most of the sample.

It was our intention to interview the entire population of dropouts. As it turned out, there were 205 African-American male dropouts the first semester of the 1989-90 school term. Our study sample is comprised of 105 of these 205 dropouts.   Further, 79 dropouts were actually interviewed and 26 relatives were interviewed for dropouts who were in detention centers, the job corps, or other states. To prevent the 26 relatives from dis- torting the research data, they were only asked background questions, such as number of siblings, that we were certain they knew. Hence, our quantitative data, as well as narrative data, are accurate.   Appropriate quantitative data were taken only from the 79 males and 26 relatives while other quantitative data were taken only from the 79 dropouts to whom we talked and the narrative data was taken only from the 79 males and two mothers. The remaining 100 respondents could not be located.When we went to the addresses provided by the Norfolk Public School System, neighbors and friends told us the families had moved and they did not know their whereabouts. Nevertheless, we were able to get an adequate sample. If we include the 26 relatives, we have interview data from over 50 percent of the sample and if we include only the 79 respondents with whom we talked, we have interview data from 39 percent of the entire dropout population. As we have explained, there was no reason to exclude the data of the 26 relatives; hence, the dropout segment of this study is about 105 African-American males who dropped out of high school.

Upon completion of the dropout data collection procedure, we wrote a letter to the Superintendent of Schools and the Director of Research, Testing and Statistics, informing them of the outstanding cooperation we received from the high school dropout specialist and high school dropouts.

The Stayins

After preparing the interview schedule for the dropouts, Briggs and I agreed to expand the study by administering a questionnaire to all the male seniors in the five high schools the first semester of the 1989-90 school term. We believed it to be valuable to compare African-American male and white male stayins with African-American male dropouts to find out what kept them in school until near the end of the first semester of their senior year. This would give us some clues as to how to keep other African-American and white males in high school. Secondly, we were interested in determining what caused some African-American males to drop out of the same five schools in which there were African-American seniors. We also desired to know whether there were different reasons that maintained the two races in school until their senior year. The dropouts and stayins comparative study, we reasoned, would expand our understanding of factors that kept both races in school. Stayins of one race could learn something from stayins of another race. In effect, along with studying the deviant, we would study the successful. Such a broad perspective would provide us with a better understanding of high school males. From this perspective, we believed that educational policy could be derived that would help all males remain in high school.

This second stage of the retention project was more involved. Permission was obtained from the Superintendent of the Norfolk Public School System with the recommendation that we obtain permission from the Director of the Norfolk Public Schools Department of Research, Testing and Statistics and each of the five high school principals to conduct a questionnaire study. After I developed the questionnaire that includes most of the same questions asked the dropouts, we submitted it to the Director of Research, Testing and Statistics, and the five principals. In turn, the director determined whether the high school principals would cooperate. First, the principals reviewed the questionnaire and suggested three changes: omission of the students' names from the questionnaire, omission of the name of the students' particular school, and a syntax problem in one of the questions. I made the changes and resubmitted copies to the Director and principals who approved it.

The next stage in the stayin research process was to schedule a research period at the five high schools. After talking with the principals, we agreed that more students, of all races, are likely to attend school on Wednesday than on Monday and Friday (the only other days we had available). Therefore, the questionnaire was completed by the seniors present on the Wednesday chosen for their school. The questionnaire was administered during the first bell in all five high schools in the cafeteria; in one school it was administered during the first bell in an auditorium. Because all the senior male students were administered the same questionnaire on the same day of the week and at the same time of day, we believe this contributed to comparable respondents; that is, they all were likely to manifest similar enthusiasm at the same time of the week, location, and time of day.

On each research day, after the students were assembled in the research setting that included a microphone system, the guidance counselors in three schools, the assistant principal in the fourth school, and the principal at the fifth school called for attention and introduced me. I spent five to seven minutes explaining to the African-American and white male stayins how to complete the questionnaire, the interpretation of the questions, and why we were conducting the survey. To say a word about the atmosphere, students did not converse with each other about the questions, though at times, they laughed about what they were reading. This further insured us of getting the opinions of each respondent. Moreover, while the senior males were completing the questionnaires, Briggs and I walked between the tables and around in the room to interpret any question that was still not clear to a few of the respondents. Our goal was to make certain that each student had the same interpretation of the questions to increase the accuracy of the study.

When the students had completed the forms, we collected the questionnaires and I returned to the microphone and thanked the young men for their outstanding cooperation and wished them a successful senior year and career. It was then time for the next bell (class period). They were dismissed by the school representative in charge of the research session to go to their second bell classes. We thanked the school representatives for the orderly research session and left.

When the seniors in all five high schools had been surveyed, I wrote a thank you letter to the superintendent, director of research, testing, and statistics, and five principals, thanking them for their splendid cooperation.

A Documentary Video

While completing the interviews with the high school dropouts and high school seniors, we began the third stage of the research project, a video. I contacted dropouts to participate in the video documentary and they were not hard to obtain. In the meantime, I contacted Dr. Frank Sellew, an assistant superintendent of the Norfolk Public Schools, to get permission to obtain seniors in the survey to also participate in the documentary. Immediately, he made such request to the principals in writing and sent me a copy of the letter. Each principal, including the principal of the Norfolk Technical and Vocational School, Mr. William Davis, supplied names and telephone numbers of possible candidates. We originally filmed twelve individuals, and settled on six students for a more detailed presentation. We chose two high school dropouts, two high school graduates: one student who became a draftsman and another is a hospital employee while attempting to get admitted to a vocational school. The other two respondents are now college freshmen; one is at Norfolk State University in Norfolk, Virginia and the second is at The College of William and Mary, Williamsburg, Virginia.

Paula Clark Briggs did all the filming while I interviewed the respondents. Once the filming was completed, I wrote the script and narrative and narrated the program and Briggs edited it. When we completed the documentary, we sent a copy to two nationally acclaimed experts for them to conclude the documentary. They were asked to answer three questions: (1) What is your assessment of the young men's views in this documentary concerning the causes and solutions to African-American males dropping out of high school (2) How do these findings relate to findings in other US cities about African-Americans and (3) How can the findings in this program be used to help retain all male students, regardless of race or ethnic group, in high school?

Even though we had learned a great deal in the interview and questionnaire data, the documentary provided greater insight on the status of high school African-American males inside and outside the high school and further enlightened the writing process. As has been shown, the methods employed to gather data for this book were conducted in three stages, which we consider worth the hundreds of hours invested. Even though my colleague Paula Clark Briggs was involved in helping to collect interview and questionnaire data, she opted to stay only with the documentary. Hence, with the insightful suggestions and editorial assistance of colleagues, especially Dr. James Nolan, Director of the Social Science Research Laboratory, Norfolk State University, Ms. Ruth Rose, teacher at Hunter College, City University of New York, and Dr. Alton Thompson, Professor of Sociology, at the Agricultural and Technical State University, Greensboro, North Carolina, it was my task to write this book.

In Summary

The sample comprises the second component of the methodology. As mentioned earlier the dropout sample is comprised of 105 (51 percent) of the 205 African-American males who dropped out of the Norfolk, Virginia high schools the first semester of the 1989-90 school year. In effect, we interviewed 79 dropouts (38.5 percent) and 26 relatives. All narrative is based on the 79 dropouts and two mothers.

As indicated the sample also included male high school seniors. There were 639 seniors in the five Norfolk High Schools the first semester of the 1989-90 school term. Of this number 404 were present on the day we administered the questionnaire in their high schools. Thus, we collected data from 63 percent of the total number of male seniors in the five high schools. Of the 235 seniors absent on the day of the survey, many of them were working on jobs obtained through the school or attending classes at the Norfolk Technical and Vocational Center.

A word about the total research process. It was perhaps the most enjoyable experience that I have participated in over the last quarter of a century. This was made possible by the professionalism at every level in the Norfolk Public School System. It was evident from the Superintendent to the students, including the dropouts. And the only difficulty was the numerous trips to locate a dropout only to find that he was not available.

Data collection among the high school seniors began in November, 1989 and lasted until March, 1990, but only five different weeks were involved. On the other hand, the dropout study began February, 1990 and ended August, 1990. The documentary data collection process was begun in March, 1991 and completed the summer of 1991.

Data from all three studies have been used to describe and analyze the behavior of white and African-American male stayins and African-American dropouts in the five Norfolk, Virginia High Schools.

PART III AFRICAN-AMERICAN MALE HIGH SCHOOL DROPOUTS

Chapter 1 Profile of High School Dropouts

The purpose of this chapter is to describe the background of high school dropouts. It includes information about the dropouts and their families. Understanding the background of students can be a deterrent to dropping out of school. The background characteristics of the African-American males in this study were a clear signal that they were potential dropouts. If these traits had been considered important, preventive measures could have been taken to maintain the former students in high school. This requires guidance counselors to know their students and prevent problems before they develop. Because guidance counselors are a bridge between advisees and their school and family, they are considered to be as important as teachers in preventing students from dropping out of school. There were several traits of the dropouts that informed the counselors that their advisees were experiencing difficulty in school.

Personal Traits

Age

The age of the respondents as shown in Table 1-1 was one indication that the students were potential dropouts. That is, they were a relatively old population for their grades. For example, the dropouts ranged in age from fifteen to twenty years. We found that more than one out of four, 28.6 percent, was under seventeen years old and 54.3 percent of the respondents were age seventeen and younger while 31.4 percent were age eighteen and 14.3 percent were ages nineteen and twenty. In reality, 45.3 percent of the dropouts should have graduated and an alarming percentage was beyond the normal age of graduation. It appears that schools have the responsibility of teaching and graduating their students rather than allowing them to drop out after they reach graduation age.

TABLE 1-1: Age of African-American Males
High School Dropouts

Age	Percent
Seventeen and Younger	54.3
Eighteen	31.4
Nineteen and Twenty	14.3

As indicated in Table 1-2, the dropouts left school in grades nine to twelve. There was a considerable gap in the dropout rate between the lower two grades and the higher two grades. Thus, 86.6 percent of the dropouts were in grades nine and ten while 13.4 percent were in the upper two grades with 10.5 percent in the twelfth grade when they dropped out of school. These findings seem to suggest that the most difficult work is with students in the ninth and tenth grade. The ninth grade appears especially critical with almost three-fourths of the dropouts leaving then. Overall, the ninth, tenth, and twelfth grades were vulnerable years for the high school dropouts. Nevertheless, it is the ninth grade that claims atten-

TABLE 1-2: Grades African-American Males
Dropped out of High School

Grade	Percent
Ninth	71.4
Tenth	15.2
Eleventh	2.9
Twelfth	10.5

tion. In effect, this is the year that students are making the transition from middle school to high school. This transitional period is difficult and needs close monitoring by the administration, counselors, and teachers. Thus, schools need to put its best teachers and counselors with ninth grade students or the first year of high school. These personnel should be dedicated to helping students make a successful transition from a smaller to a larger school. This includes behavioral skills as well as classroom content that should have been learned, but for one reason or another was not learned in middle school. School success and a favorable attitude will help ninth graders stay in school. This is the basis for maintaining and graduating them from high school. Interestingly, the respondents tended to stay in school during the eleventh grade. Hence, once students conquer the ninth and tenth grades, they seem fairly well adjusted in the eleventh grade. Yet more than 10 percent of the respondents dropped out of school in the twelfth grade.This suggests that counseling,classroom,home,and community assistance must be steady even though students have completed the eleventh grade.

Age and Grade

A broader perspective is provided when the data are presented by grade and age (see Table 1-3).Assuming that a child begins the first grade at age 6, it is easy to project a "normal" grade equivalency for different ages. Thus, 15 year olds would be expected to be in the ninth grade while 16, 17, and 18 year olds would be in the tenth, eleventh, and twelfth grades respectively. Persons older than 18 years would be assumed to have completed high school. The data show that most of the dropouts were behind such an educational progression. All of the 15 year olds were in the ninth grade when they dropped out but the other age groups show some degree of discrepancy. For the 16 year olds the expected grade equivalency is tenth but all who dropped out of school at age 16 were in the ninth grade. While the 17 year olds would be projected to be in the eleventh grade more than 90 percent were below this level and more than three fourths were in the ninth grade. For the 18 year olds only 6 percent were in the twelfth grade and 90 percent were two grades behind. These findings indicate that one of the problems the African-American males faced in high school was being in the incorrect grade for their age. This adversely affected their behavior and decision to drop out of high school. Based on the findings in this study, it seems clear that achievement on the right grade level and good behavior in the classroom prevent students from dropping out of school.

TABLE 1-3: Grade and Age of African-American Male
High School Dropouts

Grade	Age					
	15	16	17	18	19	20
9	100.0	100.0	77.8	60.6	21.4	100.0
10	0.0	0.0	14.8	30.3	14.3	0.0
11	0.0	0.0	3.7	3.0	7.1	0.0
12	100.0	0.0	3.7	6.0	57.1	0.0

Attitudes

We asked other questions to get a comprehensive profile of the high school dropouts. For example, we desired to know their inner self--their personality--conceptualized for them as emotions and behaviors. We found that 40 percent stated their attitude had contributed to them dropping out of school. Consequently, good citizenship should be taught in social studies classes. African-American males should not be allowed to demonstrate negative attitudes. These attitudes are likely to hinder their success in all settings, including the school. As shown in Table 1-4, we turned to the essence of their personality. It was determined that they were almost evenly divided between being leaders and followers. The findings suggest that about half of the respondents could possibly be influenced by others. A concerted effort should be made by the family, school, and church to help African-American males become independent thinkers and actors. When this occurs, they are far less likely to get caught in adverse situations that result in the end of their school careers before graduation. When we asked whether they were ambitious or non-caring about success in life, we found that 56.6 percent were ambitious--wanted to get ahead in life--while 24.5 percent were non-caring. As a result, more than a fourth of the respondents were not serious about their success in life.This finding indicates that health, physical education, and social studies classes need to teach the whole person to circumvent non-caring attitudes.

Even though more teaching is needed in the school, family and church, the respondents cannot be placed into one category. A large percentage still had hope of achieving in life while less than half that percentage is non-caring about what life holds for them. Hope far exceeds hopelessness. In fact, even those who were non-caring cannot be said to be hopeless; the only conclusion that we can draw is that if life is good that will be marvelous, if not, they will attempt to deal with it. Yet, the non-caring respondents should have had someone at home or in the school, church, and community to touch their lives; these African-American males should not be non-caring. Those of any race interested in volunteer work are encouraged to link themselves with high schools, especially with the students at risk of dropping out, and help them develop a caring attitude. Such attitude might encourage them to stay in school. And the at risk ambitious students need guidance and direction for their lives and personality. In other words, the ambitious student who is not successful in the classroom is likely to find deviant ways in school or away from school to realize success. Hence, it is important to assist ambitious students in realizing a good measure of success in school, especially in the classroom and in extra-curricular activities.

One related question centered on whether the respondents had a domineering or submissive attitude.We found that 34.9 percent had a domineer-

TABLE l-4: Attitudes of African-American
Male High School Dropouts

Type of Attitude	Percent
Ambitious	56.6
Leadership	44.3
Followship	41.5
Domineering	34.9
Submissive	34.9
Non-Caring	24.5

ing attitude and 34.9 had a submissive attitude. Again, the submissive respondents were at risk of being influenced adversely by peers and the domineering students were at risk of not being tactful enough, under what
they called unfair school circumstances, to successfully negotiate life and
high school.   What we must conclude is that high school dropouts need
some help with enhancing their personality. They should have a leadership attitude that enables them to make decisions for themselves.   When
the personality of the African-American male is refined, he is likely to stay
in school and not be a follower who gets into trouble in and out of school;
nor will he be domineering. Instead, he will be tactful and know how to
love himself enough to stay in school because he knows the stakes are
high.

We asked one final question somewhat related to personality: Are you a
father? We found that 79.3 percent were not fathers while 20.7 percent
were fathers. Indeed, this could have had some bearing on attitude and
dropping out of school. Hence, a related job for those who volunteer to
save African-American males is to see that the young men are programmed
emotionally and behaviorally to refrain from risking fatherhood. It seems
certain from my studies of single parents (Barnes 1987) that eliminating single fatherhood is important to preventing a sizeable number of African-
American male students from dropping out of school. Even when the males
do not support the mother of their child, being a parent damages their personality and often causes them to lose interest in school. On the other hand,
there is a small number of young male parents who work hard to succeed
in spite of parenthood.

Educational Goals

We asked the respondents what they had in mind educationally? (see
Table 1-5). Was dropping out of school the end of their school career? According to 7.5 percent, their education had ended with dropping out of
high school. Yet the vast majority had educational goals. For example, 28.8
percent of the dropouts planned to get a high school diploma and the same
percentage aimed to earn a college degree; and 22.5 percent expected to
earn a GED. In general, the dropouts planned to continue their education.
Education is not disvalued despite the fact that these youth dropped out
of school. This finding suggests that the dropouts, with the correct assistance, could have succeeded in high school. In essence, dropouts are not
adverse to education; on the contrary, when they get out on the streets,
they see the value of an education. The problem is that they are not helped
to realize early enough the disadvantage of dropping out of school. These
findings continue to suggest the need for training. Because parents often
do not know how to provide such training, it is important for the church

and school to help them out.

TABLE 1-5: Educational Goals of African-American
Male High School Dropouts

Educational Goals	Percent
High Diploma	28.8
College Eduation	28.8
GED	22.5
End of Education	7.5
Trade School	5.0
Indefinite	5.0
Medical Doctor	1.2
Associate Degree	1.2

Occupational Goals

Another concern was the occupational outlook of the respondents. Without an education, they were limited in their occupational attainment. When asked about their occupational goals,we found that the high school dropouts varied (see Table 1-6).   For example, more than 24 percent did not have any occupational goals This is an alarming finding. Will these men spend the rest of their life jobless? Will they depend on African-American women to take care of them? What is their occupational future? They needed the work ethics value instilled in them while in school. Yet, the remainder had set occupational goals. The largest percent planned-white collar occupations and 10.1 percent planned to enter the military. Al-

TABLE 1-6: Occupational Goals of African-American
Male High School Dropouts

Occupations	Percent
White Collar	38.0
Blue Collar	25.3
Indefinite	24.1
Military	10.1
Professional	2.5

together over 75 percent of the respondents had occupational goals. Desiring to work, they needed at least a high school diploma.

The Meaning of Success

What seemed to lie ahead for the respondents? To get some reasonable understanding of this question, they were asked what success meant to them (see Table 1-7). In the order of frequency, success to the respondents meant getting a good job (86.3 percent), getting a good paying job (84.5

TABLE 1-7: The Meaning of Success to African-American Male High School Dropouts	
Types of Success	Percent
A Good Job	86.3
A Good Paying Job	84.5
High School Diploma	80.7
Excellent Work	80.2
House Purchase	76.8
College Degree	63.3
Compatible Friends	60.5
Car Purchase	55.8
A Family	47.5

percent), earning a high school diploma or its equivalent (80.7 percent), excellent work on some job (80.2 percent), buying a home (76.8 percent), obtaining a college degree (63.3 percent), having compatible friends (60.5 percent) owning a car (55.8 percent), and getting married and then having children (47.5 percent). It is apparent that success for these dropouts agrees with that of mainstream America. There is one important step missed in their lives and that is a viable education. Rather than drop students from school rolls and suspend and expel them, ways should be found to educate African-American males in the school setting.

The Family

Residence

Understanding the dropouts also required knowledge of their family life.

For example, What is the living arrangement of the respondents? Do they live with both parents? (see Table 1-8). It was determined that 6.6 percent lived with their father as the only parent, 58.5 percent lived with their mother as the only parent and 23.6 percent lived with both parents, and the remaining ll.3 percent lived with other persons. Nevertheless, it is clear that in general the respondents were from broken homes; moreover, this ties in with the most important person in their lives. Their mothers tended to be that person as well as the person with whom they lived.

TABLE l-8: Residence of African-American Male High School Dropouts

Lives with	Percent
Mother	58.5
Both Parents	23.6
Other Person	11.3
Father	6.6

The Most Important Person in Their Life

Another trait in their family life concerns the most important person in the respondents' life (see Table 1-9). As we expected, a large percentage (67.0) indicated their mothers were the most important person in their life and 2.8 percent noted their grandmother as the most important person in their life. Hence, 69.8 percent were closer to a female than male kinsman. Because only 3.8 percent were closer to their father than anybody else, in

TABLE l-9: The Most Important Person to African-American Male High School Dropouts

Most Important Person	Percent
Mother	67.0
Other Person	17.9
Father	3.8
Older Sibling	3.8
Not Identified	3.8
Grandmother	2.8
Grandfather	0.9

effect, the respondents had generally bonded with their mothers rather than with their fathers or other members of their family. A large percentage of the respondents had seen the world from a maternal or other female kinswoman's perspective.The question these findings raise is: Would a two parent family have made a difference? Perhaps some students would have dropped out of school, but we believe that fewer would have been dropouts if both parents had been living together. In other words, some fathers may have been more influential than mothers.

The usual question following a respondent's response that his mother was the most important person in his life was why do you consider this person to be your closest friend? According to the respondents, they bonded with their mothers for varied reasons. One reason was that mothers served as confidants. Some of the respondents explained that they could talk with their mothers about anything. A few of the respondents went so far as to say that not only did their mothers talk with them about anything, but they understood things from their point of view while at the same time they presented their opinion. They gave advice about attending school, type of desirable friends, and personal problems. When mother and son disagreed,the respondents did what they considered right. The respondents especially liked being able to discuss their problems with their mothers and get advice. One respondent perhaps put his view of his mother best:

> I look up to my mother. I admire her hardwork and dedication to our family. No matter what obstacles we come up against, with love she keeps the family together. When one of us is having a problem, she talks with us, tells us what to do, and guides us lovingly. Then, I feel a whole lot better. I believe that what she tells me is right. I know she wouldn't say anything to hurt me.

This respondent appreciated the love his mother used to guide the family. Consequently, a lack of family love did not cause him to leave school.

The love of many respondents' mothers went beyond their appreciation of their loving and leadership attitude. It also included a hugging and kissing relationship wherein they told their mothers they loved them. In turn, the respondents' mothers told them they were their "baby." Rather than telling a teenage male he is a baby, perhaps it would be more beneficial to say that he is mama's achieving son. Moreover, many of these women were without husbands, and it is likely they substituted the love they received from their sons for love they missed in a courtship or marriage relationship. Consequently, sweet words, hugs, and kisses were likely to result in mothers being more lenient toward the respondents than success allows. Indeed, if this is the case, mother-son relationships help put African-American males at risk in the Norfolk public high schools.

The respondents also considered their mother the most important person in their life, because she was a great motivator.As long as possible,she motivated them to attend school and pushed them to succeed, go to night school, and obtain a GED.Some mothers of these respondents sent letters to the officials in the school system to get their sons transferred to a different school and accepted back in school. And a few respondents' mother helped them with their homework.

The respondents also considered their mother the most important person in their life because she provided for them economically. In their words, she gave them a place to sleep, food to eat, and clothes to wear, and did their laundry. In other words, they stated that she was always there when they needed her. This is an interesting point.The respondents were socialized into depending on a female, their mother, to take care of them economically. One must speculate about the long run effect of mothers providing a living for their children from birth to age eighteen. Does this not weaken the African-American male's determination to go to school and become self-sufficient? Does it not make him rely on girlfriends and wives for economic support? We propose here that some mothers who served as the only or main breadwinners trained their sons to depend on rather than to support women. Because these mothers either were without spouses or their husbands did not take an active role in childrearing, it is important that the family, church, community, and school stress the breadwinning responsiblity of males, especially African-American males. Resocialization can move them away from dependency on women to support of women. Equally important, there needs to be a greater countertrend from single parenthood (divorced and unwed) to two parent African-American families.

There are still other reasons that explain why the respondents considered their mothers to be the most important person in their lives. One of these reasons was that mothers were tolerant of their sons' unproductive behavior. For example, according to the respondents, mothers "put up" with them staying out late at night, sleeping late in the morning and afternoon, and being unemployed. Like their breadwinning role, it appears that the mother's tolerance of hanging out and "laying around" failed to prepare the respondents for staying in school and becoming disciplined to study and achieve. Rather than helping the respondents, these mothers contributed to their failure to remain in high school. It is not enough to profile this situation, but it invites an urgent solution.

Siblings

Still another line of family inquiry concerned the number of siblings of the dropouts (see Table 1-10). We found that 23.6 percent did not have any brothers and 18.9 percent did not have any sisters. The largest percent

(27.4) had one brother and one sister (32.l). In general, they had either a
brother or sister or both. Only 1.0 had no siblings.

TABLE l-10: Siblings of African-American Male
High School Dropouts

Number	Brothers	Sisters
None	23.6	18.9
One	27.4	32.1
Two	22.6	28.3

Birth order

To further understand the African-American dropouts, we inquired
about their birth order (see Table l-ll). We found that a majority of them
were first born (30.5 percent) or second born (22. 8 percent), and 16.2 percent were third born. In general, they were the older children in the family.
In seminars and other programs, African-American parents, must be taught
to rear their first child as successfully as they rear younger children.

TABLE l-11: Birth Order of African-American
Male High School Dropouts

Birth Order	Per Cent
First	30.5
Second	22.8
Third	16.2
Other	28.6
No Response	1.9

Siblings' School Dropout History

Did the respondents' siblings drop out of school? (see Table l-l2). The
respondents noted that 60.4 percent did not have any brothers and 75.5
percent did not have any sisters who dropped out of school. Nevertheless,
the percentages suggest considerable dropping out of school in the respondents' families.Hence, 34.9 percent had experienced at least one
brother and l8.9 percent had at least one sister to drop out of school.

The next question concerned the grades in which the respondents' siblings dropped out of school (see Table l-l3). We found that the largest percentage of their male siblings dropped out in the ninth, tenth, and eleventh

TABLE 1-12: African-American Male High School
Dropouts with Siblings Who Dropped
Out of School

School Status	Brothers	Sisters
Dropped Out	34.9	18.9
Did not Drop Out	60.4	75.5
No Response	4.7	5.6

grades; hence, in each of these grades, 21.3 percent of their male siblings dropped out of school. Likewise,the largest percent of their female siblings

TABLE 1-13: Grades African-American Male
Siblings Dropped Out of School

Grade	Brothers	Sisters
5	2.1	0.0
8	6.4	0.0
9	21.3	12.5
10	21.3	20.8
11	21.3	25.0
12	14.9	12.5
No Response	12.3	29.2

dropped out in the ninth (12.5), tenth (20.8), eleventh (25.8), and twelfth grades (12.5) Moreover, a small percentage of the respondents' male siblings dropped out between grades five and eight while none of their female siblings dropped out in these same grades.

Parental Schooling

The family profile of the respondents also included their parents' schooling (see Table 1-14). A considerable percentage of the fathers (10.5) and mothers (9.5) had less than high school training. Also, it was found that 39 percent were from families whose fathers had a high school education; and 35.2 percent of their mothers were high school graduates. Among the fathers, 5.7 percent had some college training while 17.1 percent of the mothers had some college training. Further, 3.8 percent of the fathers and 2.9 percent of the mothers had a college degree.

TABLE 1-14: Education of African-American Male
High School Dropouts' Parents

Education Level	Fathers	Mothers
Less Than High School	10.5	9.5
Some High School	14.3	27.6
High School Graduate	39.0	35.2
Some College	5.7	17.1
College Graduate	3.8	2.9
Unknown	26.7	7.6

Parental Employment

Upon finding out the education of the respondents' parents, we asked about their work (see Table 1-15). And found that 64.2 percent of the fathers worked and 63.2 percent of the mothers worked. In all other cases (35.8 percent), the respondents either stated their father was unemployed or they did not know his work status; on the other hand, 31.1 percent stated that their mothers did not work while 5.7 percent were uncertain. A size-able number of respondents had working fathers; yet, more than one-third did not. All African-American men ought to be either in school or at work. This should be the goal of the African-American leaders, community, and government.

TABLE 1-15: Work Status of African-American Male
High School Dropouts' Parents

Employment Status	Fathers	Mothers
Employed	64.2	63.2
Unemployed	13.2	31.1
Unknown	22.6	5.7

Parental Occupations

We determined the types of work the dropouts' parents did and divided the occupations into a number of categories (see Table 1-16). Of the respondents identifying their parents' occupations, the largest percent of the fathers were in blue collar jobs, both skilled and unskilled. The unskilled fathers worked as log cutters, grocery store helpers, furniture movers, and as a janitor. On the other hand, the skilled blue collar fathers worked as pipefitters, metal smiths, truck and bus drivers, hair stylists, mechanics, welders, long shoremen, short shoremen, forklifters, postmen, roofers, plumbers, plasterers, and a police officer. Also, 14 percent of the fathers were employed in white collar occupations. They were administrators, supervisors, managers, and a computer specialist. However, the work status of the fathers of some respondents was either unemployment or unknown.

The dropouts' mothers were also employed in varied occupations (see Table l-16). The largest percentage (24.2) was white collar workers. They were managers, salespersons, a financial officer, clerks, secretaries, and a computer analyst. The second largest percentage (17.8) of the dropouts' mothers was blue collar workers. The unskilled mothers did domestic, laundry, janitorial, and meat wrapping work while the skilled mothers worked as hair stylists, bus drivers, cooks, dieticians,and a sheet metallist.

TABLE l-16: Occupation of African-American Male
High School Dropouts' Parents

Occupations	Fathers	Mothers
Professional	7.0	16.9
White Collar	14.0	24.2
Blue Collar	35.0	17.8
Service	0.0	5.1
Housewife	0.0	0.4
Military	6.2	0.0
Retired	0.8	0.0
Employed	14.0	11.9
Unemployed	10.7	9.7
No Response	12.3	14.0

School Disciplinary Experiences

Turning from the family, we asked what was school like from the perspective of the respondents? (See Table l-l7). They informed this study that they experienced a good deal of disciplinary action. For example, 78.1 percent received suspension letters and 19.0 percent received expulsion letters. However, 13.3 percent of the dropouts did not receive any expulsions or suspensions. It thus appears that suspensions and expulsions influenced, at least in part, the respondents' decision to leave school. Apparently school was not an attractive experience. African-American males need to be told as early as the fifth grade that white racism and Black racism aim to get rid of African-American males with certain dispositions and they should fight back by refusing to do everything they are accused of.

TABLE 1-17: Disciplinary Experiences of African-American Male High School Dropouts

Disciplinary Action	Percent
Suspension Letters	78.1
Expulsion Letters	19.0
No Disciplinary Letters	13.3

Yet, there is more that should be known about the respondents' disciplinary experience. We asked who was responsible for them becoming a disciplinary problem (See Table 1-18). Forty seven percent accused themselves of being responsible for becoming a disciplinary problem. Moreover, 20 percent indicated that teachers were responsible for their disciplinary behavior. School officials (10 percent) were also accused of helping students become a disciplinary problem; and other people (8 per-

TABLE 1-18: Persons Responsible for African-American Male High School Dropouts' Disciplinary Problems

Individual	Percent
Self	47.0
Teachers	12.0
School Officials	10.0
Students	5.0
Another Person	2.0
Friend	1.0
No Response	23.0

cent) contributed to the respondents' disciplinary behavior. These findings suggest that a large percentage of persons intervened in the lives of the respondents. Hence teachers, school officials, and acquaintances should be careful about the impact they make on African-American high school males.

Our next question centered on the respondents' perspective of the school's action in their disciplinary behavior. Approximately two-thirds of the respondents stated that the school was not fair in handling their case. Surely, high school students ought to perceive the school's disciplinary system as fair. Indeed, this is an alarming percentage that encourages us to request that schools in the Norfolk Public School System review and improve their disciplinary policies, procedures, and actions.

We learned from the in-depth narratives that suspension and expulsion were primarily responsible for the respondents dropping out of high school. Yet, we sought to determine whether family finances, family need for them to work, and personal illness contributed to their decision to drop out. And, unexpectedly, we found that none of these was important. We did, however, find that dropping out because they wanted a job or to work at the same time they went to school contributed to the respondents' decision to drop out of school (29.5 percent) and that the desire to go into the military (20.5) also contributed to the dropout status. In this group, there were those who figured they could study for the GED, get a diploma in night school, or earn a GED in the job corp. In effect, African-American males who do not have to work ought to be taught to study while they are in school and work after graduation. They should realize they have a life-time to work and only twelve years to get a public school education. This is a matter of helping African-American males get their priorities straightened out.

In conclusion, society should be ridded of a high school dropout problem. It appears this problem can be overcome among African-American males with help from varied sources. Specifically, students, the home, church, and school can work together to keep African-American males in school. For African-American males, such task should begin in kindergarten. At any level of schooling, African-American males can become a dropout but they stay in school until a later date. Indeed, many of the African-American males in this study were dropouts in high school before they made it official. Frequently, they became a dropout when they had disciplinary problems and received suspension and expulsion letters. They made it official during suspension and expulsion or soon after the periods ended.

Chapter 2 Personal Reasons for Dropping Out of High School

Dropping out or being put out of high school can not be attributed to the home, school, or individual. Instead, it is a complex problem that involves all the major institutions as well as the students. We begin by discussing personal behavior of students that contributed to discontinuation of high school.

Drugs

Drugs were one reason the respondents dropped out of high school. They were sold by students and others at lunch time outside the school buildings and between classes by students in the men's restrooms. Some of the former students discontinued going to school because their friends were either drug users or entrepreneurs and they feared their resistance to drugs would cause them to lose their friends. For example, one former student stated that if it had not been for the sale and use of drugs in his high school, which he avoided, he would have graduated rather than dropped out of high school.

There was a definite pattern among some drug users. They felt disinterested in school and went home at lunch time. Hooking resulted in suspension, increased disinterest in school, and discontinuation of their education. One of the respondents left high school because he was in the drug crowd and got in trouble with the police. Drug dealing enabled him to make money and buy expensive clothing; school became unimportant.

At least one male dropped out of high school because his mother was on drugs. This former student stated, "My mother was on crack. If she had stayed off crack, I would still be in high school." According to the former student, he had never used or sold drugs, yet the school officials became suspicious that he was selling drugs. The suspicion developed when he had, in his possession, a cordless telephone. In actuality, he says, the telephone belonged to a friend and he used it to call girls. The school officials attempted to take the telephone and beeper, but he told them that he would not give it to them. Needless to say, he was suspended. In this case, the respondent says that he was suspected of behavior that he totally rejected. Perhaps school administrators can determine the use a particular student makes of a cordless telephone before assuming the student is involved in drugs. A thorough investigation should precede punishment of any sort. Instead of drugs, the ultimate reason that the respondent left school was fighting. Hence, the school overlooked the student's problem and lost its holding power on an African-American male.

Because resistance to drug sales and use of drugs lead to black attrition in high school, we asked the dropouts and putouts for solutions to the drug problem in high schools. One former student related several solutions that encompass all the major suggestions. He recommended that schools use graduates of the particular high school and young policemen, as undercover agents, to mingle in male restrooms between classes and outside the gymnasium at lunch time. A related recommendation is that monitors be placed in the high school men's restrooms. He got the idea from 21 Jump Street. Another solution the former student offered is to openly employ policemen to patrol the school grounds. He also recommended random testing for drug usage and imprisonment of the guilty to serve as an example and hindrance to drug use. Suspensions, in his opinion, were not the answer. They were seen as merely a technique to perpetuate the drug problem rather than eliminate it. Then, the former student turned to a learning approach to solving the drug problem in the Norfolk high schools. In his opinion, schools should sponsor anti-drug programs (assemblies) four times a year that stress the effects of drugs on the brain and how they cause death. Included in these assemblies, according to the respondent, should be dropouts who have "kicked the habit." These persons should relate their experiences and the seriousness of the problem as well as the advantages of staying in high school and earning a diploma. Also, he suggested modeling, in high school, as a means of halting the escalation and use of drugs. High school athletes, he believes, should be the models. He stated that, based on regular urine tests, schools should allow only the drug free athletes to participate in school sports. In effect, the prestigious high school athletes would serve as anti-drug models; and he believes that many other students would imitate them.

Fighting

Violence,especially fighting,is another major behavior in African-American male attrition in the Norfolk high schools. Elimination of fighting among African-American males, alone, would greatly increase the retention of high school males. It seems necessary for all community institutions, especially, the family,church, and school,to put an end to violence by the high school African-American male. Fighting is not just among themselves, but in the Norfolk High Schools, African-American males are involved in inter-racial fights as well.

Inter-racial Fighting

We will discuss inter-racial fights first because they were less frequent than fights among African-American males. Yet, inter-racial fights appear to be a problem that deserves particular attention. Several of the respondents left school because they were suspended or expelled for fighting white males. The former students fought with white males because, in their opinion, they appeared to consider themselves a notch above African-American males. For example, a former student said, "We don't take much off each other and we take less off white boys because they are considered precious. We let them know they are not precious." When asked how they arrived at the conclusion that white males consider themselves "precious," they said that, in their opinion, white males believe they are better than African-American males which disturbs them. Evidence of the "preciousness" of white male students was felt when they greeted white males who failed to return their greeting. For example, when an African-American male spoke to a white male student and he would not answer, the African-American male student responded by saying, "I know you hear me speaking." Because the white male appeared too "precious" to speak, the young African-American male fought him. This same young man related that he had another reason for fighting white male students. On one occasion, during lunch hour, a white male student called him names. He responded by telling him to leave him alone and saying that he did not want to play. Yet, the white male student continued to call him bad names. When the African-American male student became tired of hearing them, he fought the white male student, in the lunchroom, with trays and chairs. After calling the school a police state, he stated that he was surprised that the school officials did not take him from the lunchroom. Knowing that he was in trouble, after the lunch hour was over, he went home only to return the next day and get suspended too many days to pass his courses. Hence, the end of his high school career in Norfolk. Another fight occurred at the corner of a hall. An African-American male deliberately bumped up against a white male student. When asked, Why? he said, he simply wanted to do it.

In still another case, when a former student was in the school auditorium, he made a mistake and stepped on a white male's foot. As soon as it occurred, the white student began "talking smart." The African-American male student said, "You better shut your mouth before I punch you in the face." At that moment, says the former student, "the white student stood up like he wanted to do something." Even though the white student merely made a gesture that signaled his intention to fight--it quickly provoked the African-American male. That was a succesful strategy because before the white student reacted to him physically, the African-American male acted and received the punishment. Again, what African-American males must learn early about provocations in high school is that white males know they have a quick temper and defeat them through suspensions and expulsions without striking a single blow. Thus, the African-American student may win the battle, but he loses the war. And victory in the war is what is important. It is time for African-Americans to stop losing the war among young white males and learn to control themselves.

The consequence of the fight in the auditorium was grave. This fight took place at the beginning of the school year and the respondent was expelled for the remainder of the school term while the white student was not expelled. In fact, he went to school the next day. The respondent said, "I guess they let him off because he is white. I got expelled because I am Black. I got a long punishment period because I am Black." He continued by saying that " White folks get off easier for the same thing." Another former student noted, "Black people, teachers and principals, take up for white students. Every time a white and Black fight, the Black person gets more days. This is prejudice." It is necessary for white and Black teachers and administrators to nurture African-American males the same way they nurture white males. And it is obvious that African-American males recognize inequalities in the administration of school justice; yet, recognition is not enough; they must be able to keep themselves out of situations that breed injustice.

Also, it appears that white male students should be taught to avoid creating anger in African-American males.Moreover,African-American males should be taught that white high school males know how to get them punished through suspensions and expulsions. Then, African-American males while young should be taught to fight the racist system by learning how to deal with white antagonism that causes them to get suspended and miss their opportunity to get a high school education. That is, the African-American male should be taught to report all adverse behavior of white males to the administration and teachers and tactfully but forcefully insist on justice. When the school does not listen, the students, their parents, and community leaders should go to the office of the principal and other public school administrators. They should insist on justice for the perpetrator as well as for the actor. This will encourage white and African-American males to get along. Then white males will not punish African-American males by causing them to lose out on receiving a high school education and diploma.

On the basis of these findings, some white high school male students use subtle and not so subtle ways to provoke African-American males into committing behavior that leads to suspensions and expulsions. It is urgent that African-American males become fully cognizant of this and either bluff them, like whites, or be constant tattle-tales to people in authority. Also, African-American males must learn to walk away from trouble and avoid getting angry because the white male thinks he is stupid enough to fight; simply refuse to fight and end their high school career. In other words, put an end to white youthful racism.

Indeed,the relations between African-American males and white males in high school should be among the schools' top priorities. The continuous aggravation of the respondents by the subtle and not so subtle behavior of white students must have interfered with concentration on their school work and it usually resulted in the end of their high school career. One can only speculate as to whether other high school males do poorly in school because they feel they are at a disadvantage, compared to white males, and do not enjoy an equal adult classroom, hallway, and office relationship. If so, even the African-American males who graduate begin their adult career a step behind white males. That is, a majority enters the adult world with the expectation of unequal treatment which is likely to become a self-fulfilling prophecy.

We found it interesting that the respondents often spoke of school inequalities between the races. The question this raises is: Does the school set in motion inequitable treatment that African-American males often face outside the school? If institutions, such as the school, are the breeding ground for victimization of African-American males, it can help the whole society by demonstrating the same punishment for equal offenses.

Racial Fighting

As indicated earlier, not only do African-American high school males contend with interracial fights, but they also experience intra-racial fights. The latter are far more frequent because the young male students have more contact with each other than with white male students. African-American high school males fight about a number of things, including dislike for the actions of others. Offensive actions cause them to become hypersensitive. As one former student noted, "When I am hyper, I fight. If someone says the wrong thing while looking at me I fight." Even though he mostly fights with his hands, he also uses high powered weapons. He said, however, "I would be in school today with the right Mama.I am just a bad boy." It appears that all institutions, the family, community--especially the church, agencies, and school--need to prevent African-American males from becoming "bad boys."

In talking with another respondent, he explained that his brother had taught him how to fight and had given him boxing gloves. When he was younger, he and his brother boxed for hours. What this means is that when some African-American males reach high school, they are prepared to fight. This makes it more important to prevent situations that require them to utilize their previous violent training.

To further illustrate the skill of African-American males in fighting, a former student talked about himself:

> When I fought one boy,he had to get stitches in his mouth.I have a talent for fighting.I picked it up in elementary school.I am an amateur boxer.I learned to fight because I had to fight to take care of myself outside school.

Perhaps the expertise that African-American males have in fighting is most vivid in this respondent's behavior. He said:

> I know how to fight. I have a one punch action. I punch in the face.If I hit him in the right spot in the face, he'll fall. Some boys don't fall.When this happens, I have to give him more hard punches.When I see the boy that I have beaten, I don't speak to him.

This is a point that is often overlooked. Our respondents have indicated they are trained for warfare. Because of this preparation, stringent efforts must be made not to create rage in them and to defuse whatever rage develops. It is also important that community groups grab African-American high school males and defuse their rage. African-American groups in each city and county in these United States should have as one of their educational goals, the diffusion of rage in African-Americans, especially young males.

There is another element involved. In all probability, the African-American males fight each other to obtain status in their own group since it is difficult for most African-American males to obtain equal status with white males in the high school setting. We are suggesting that a better school experience would help African-American males feel better about themselves and less prone to fight their own or whites.

African-American males also fight each other about money.For example, one male student took the money belonging to a fellow student who thought the respondent had taken the money.The theft victim began fighting and took the respondent to the principal's office. According to the respondent, because both of them lived in a certain housing development in Norfolk, the disciplinary officer assumed they would fight. Indeed, this student believed that the disciplinary officer in his school had a predetermined notion that African-American males from certain neighborhoods automatically fought. Certainly, this kind of opinion ought to be dispelled from high school disciplinarian officers, because it might become a self-fulfilling prophecy; moreover,each student,regardless of neighborhood environment, ought to be judged on his own merit. Further,students should never get the notion,from administrators, that they are judged on the basis of where they live.

There were also times when the young high school students fought because of false rumors. For example, one respondent noted:

> I was a member of a small group of boys and we were dancing and rapping on a radio station.Another group called the station and said that we couldn't do this or that.And,if they saw us, they were going to get us. In the meantime, a Black girl served as a go be-

tween. One night, my friends and I saw the other group at a base-ball game and fought them. Later we asked questions and learned that all the news the girl had brought us was lies.

This is indeed one case where an African-American female used a subtle technique to cause African-American males to get involved in violence. This suggests that African-American females should be taught the importance of staying out of males' interpersonal relations.

Then, of course, there were dropouts who left school because they wanted to avoid fights. For example, one respondent did not belong to a gang, but while he was in school, two gangs were shooting. As a result, he would not go to school; yet, the judge ordered him back to school. He went to school two days; there were confrontations and the students threatened him. He has not been back to school. This was his position with the gangs. One gang was on one side of the street and another was on the other side of the street. He partially grew up with the gang on one side of the street and later moved to the other side of the street and finished growing up. As a result, he did not belong to either gang and was caught in the middle.

On the other side of the problem, there were some African-American high school males who were putting quick tempers aside and looked out for their personal interest. For example, one of these males provided this description of himself and his friends:

> I have a temper, but not a bad temper. I am patient. My father doesn't have a temper, but Mama does. One day in gym class, we were playing basketball and I was checking-- guarding a player. He hit me and I was about to hit him, however, I had a B average and told the coach. My pride was hurt and I told him that I was going to get him back. My brothers also became angry. I saw this same fellow at an amusement place and he smiled and asked, "What are you going to do?" My friends and I walked away. He was with four other guys. I left and returned with my brothers and met them in the amusement restaurant. We fought and messed up the tables and the police broke up the fight.
>
> My brothers and I went outside the building and waited. Then, we went to the parking lot. This guy who hit me on the basketball court came to the parking lot with five other guys. We thought it was over. Instead, he hit my brother and knocked off his hat. My big brother said to me, "Do it!" As my brother suggested, I cut the boy's wrist. The police came out to the parking lot and pulled my friend off one boy. The guy that I cut on the wrist went in the

game room and my brothers and I eased out of the picture.

The police took the boy and one of my friends in a room for ques-
tioning. We left and came back to check on our friend. My brother's girlfriend told us that our friend had gone home. On our way
to the parking lot, the boy and his five friends came up in a car.
Two of them chased us in the parking lot. When those two got
tired of chasing us, they jumped in the car and two more jumped
out of the car and continued the chase.We were running and I was
afraid. In my mind, I said, Jesus, please help me!I was scared, drinking, and about to fall. My brother tapped me on my shoulder and
said come on. A car with friends who stay in a neighborhood next
to ours picked us up.That was a miracle! I think that the other
group had a baseball bat and they were trying to run over us with
the car.

The fight occurred between the ninth and tenth grades. I had a
bad ninth grade school year,grade-wise,and my behavior chang-
ed.Then, I went back in the tenth grade and did not stay long before they suspended me.

While on suspension, I got into worse trouble.For example,I went
to court today because I was riding last September in a stolen car.

I did not realize what I was getting into. I was going through the
stage of trying to look good.I must go back to court June 10, 1990.
This is my first felony.I was in jail a week. I have been learning
lately that I must get myself together.

This example of a former high school student indicates a number of needs.
First, when a student reports a problem to teachers or administrators, they
need to deal effectively with it. If this does not occur, the problem will extend beyond the school grounds and have repercussions on the students'
grades and life. For example, the life of an African-American male athlete
with a B average changed after a coach did not solve his problem. He
ended up getting suspended and the suspension-vacation allowed him to
get into worse trouble than he had experienced in high school. Should it
really be this way? If so, what indeed is the role of the coaches, counselors, teachers, and administrators? It seems that these young inexperi-
enced males could be helped by the professionals who have them as their
charge.

Quick Temper

The next logical question was why African-American males fight. The
repetitive answer was quick temper. The African-American male high

school dropouts and putouts described their temper. Gangs were one reason a few of the respondents expressed their temper through fighting. One
respondent described how the gangs worked and the nature of his temper.

> I have a quick temper and will fight. When I was in school there
> were a lot of people who wanted to fight me.There were two
> gangs.The people who wanted to fight me live in Huntersville and
> their gang was comprised of twenty Black males.I live in Park
> Place and my gang has thirty Black males.

> Our gangs fought to prove who was the badest. Park Place could
> out-fight Huntersville because we had more guns. One boy in Park
> Place got shot.As a result, Huntersville boys won't come to Park
> Place. Nobody comes to Park Place. We stay together. The police-
> men ride around, but they don't scare us. When the police see us,
> they keep going.Even when members of our gangs go to jail, they
> fight in jail.

> To give an idea of my temper-- if someone touches me, it ticks me
> off. If they grab me, that makes me mad. Even my parents don't
> do that.

The finding that gangs exist in Norfolk and that the police look the other
way are challenges for the Norfolk Police Department as well as for other
agencies and organizations, including the family, church, and school. The
police department is called upon to use its gang war strategies. Moreover,
through nurturing, the police department could have a relationship with
the gangs that makes them disband and their members return to school or
go to work.

Then, still another former student described his temper this way:

> I have a big temper.When someone pisses me off,I get devious.
> That is I use ways of paying them back that might hurt them.What
> I do, depends on the situation they put me in. The least little thing
> makes me mad. I like for things to go my way. If they don't go my
> way, I get pissed off. Not necessarily physical. However, if they
> get physical with me, I get physical.

   The situation is compounded by the finding that it was rare to find a
young man who said he did not have a quick temper. They said such
things as, "When I get fed up, I blow my top-argue." "Simple things make
me real mad and I argue. With a girl, I argue, but with a boy I fight." Also,
a few noted, "I get angry quick, especially if somebody destroys my prop-
erty," "I'm hyper," and "It makes me mad for someone to argue with me."
Another respondent said, " I have a quick temper when I am told to shut

up. A teacher told me to shut up. I told her don't tell me to shut up. I am not your son. Ask me to be quiet. I didn't appreciate being told to shut up." He knew that he would be sent to the office. As he had anticipated, the school officer took the side of the teacher. In his opinion, the school supported the teachers more than the students. The important question here is, Should teachers be supported when they tell young adult males, of any race, to shut up? I believe that it would be better to take the student's side in a case like this and help the teacher treat high school African-American males as young adults. Also, when the principal is in doubt, why not ask the students what occurred in class? Why not have an open and fair school? In a similar case, when a teacher called one of the dropouts "boy," he threw a chair at her and got suspended.

Since the respondents revealed the kinds of things that caused them to become involved in racial and inter-racial fights we can set about in the home, community, criminal justice, and school systems to help them overcome quick tempers and remove the obstacles that cause them to fight. The African-American males need a great deal of training in overcoming quick tempers.

Because a quick temper is the major cause for fights and subsequent suspensions and expulsions, we probed the matter further and sought its origin. Up-rooting the origin would be the most successful way to help African-American males avoid developing quick tempers that lead to fights. According to the respondents with quick tempers, they learned them from peers. For example,one former student who,at one time, did not have a quick temper stated, "I watched my friends and saw how they acted and I caught on. That is, I saw how they talked back to others quickly, acted violent, fought, and pushed. After I learned to have a quick temper and showed it, I got status. It made me feel important." This finding may have a lot of embedded meaning. The quick tempers in many of our former students may result from the need for status. If, indeed, this is the case, someone, including the family, community, church, or high school, has the responsibility of channeling the aggressive energies of African-American high school males into productive activities that provide positive status. In fact, African-American males deserve status at the earliest school level and throughout their school career which will make them feel good about themselves and preclude the need to search for deviant means to acquire status. African-American males desire opportunity in school the way white males receive it. Also, this case indicates the need to work with peer groups in developing positive standards.

In still another case, environment caused the development of a violent temper. Hence, a dropout student developed a temper after he and his family moved into a housing development. He got in the wrong crowd and drank liquor. Housing developments should be ridded of deviant behavior. This is the responsibility of the entire local community. African-American males have the right to grow up in desirable communities. This student's drinking begins when he started doing poorly in school and therefore signals the significance of good grades. When students are misbehaving, rather than punish them, the counseling department should find out why and help remove the cause, which is often a lack of success in the classroom and peer pressure.

Some other respondents developed quick tempers because of peer pressure. For example, one acted up and disrupted class and was physically and verbally abusive. When he was in high school, his public behavior became increasingly violent until he was placed in a residential environment. And the reason was peer pressure. The peer group must be an object of improvement.

Of course, a majority of the former students had a quick temper and reported they learned them mainly from their parents and sometimes from siblings. One high school dropout described how he learned his quick temper from his parents:

> My father and mother have a quick temper. When I was five years old, I saw Daddy with objects in his hand chasing Mama in the house. According to Grandmama,once daddy hit mama in the head with an iron.But this time,I saw him pick up a black coal stove that was about two or three feet high and chase her with it.A stroke of luck saved her. At that moment, two uncles and my grandmother drove up.Mama took my brother and me out the door to live with grandmama.Mama had already telephoned them to come and help her.After I was five years old, I never lived with my father but I had learned about a quick temper.Besides, the home and community environment in which I grew up caused me to fight.

Like the father in this story, many of the high school dropouts were angry young men. According to them, they learned their quick temper from their mother or father or from both. Because their parents had quick tempers, the family was the training ground for the quick tempers developed by the respondents. Moreover, it would be difficult for a quick tempered parent to teach his/her child not to have a quick temper. The example would likely be stronger than the precept. Thus, African-American churches, recreational centers, police departments, community organizations, fraternities, sororities,the media,and Parent and Teachers Associations should concern themselves with training parents to be good parents--even before the baby is conceived.

Study Habits

Failure to study was another important problem among the respondents. They did not study for varied reasons. Some dropouts were discouraged from studying because they did not get the grades they felt they deserved. For example, one student stated, "The lowest grades that I should have gotten were As, Bs, and Cs. On homework, a white female teacher gave me a D." Then, another student stated:

> When I got a B, I thought I deserved an A; when I got a C, I thought I deserved a B. I often thought that I deserved better grades than I received.I wish some teachers had been different.I wish that my counselor had changed my biology teacher. I took biology three times under the same teacher. Another teacher would have been better.Another teacher could have helped me clearly understand the class.

If indeed this is the case, this matter bears consideration. Lack of correct rewards for work can cause students not to study adequately and ineffective teaching compounds the problem.

Perhaps low grades were one way some teachers compensated African-American males for disrupting their class. If so, such teachers need strengthening through teaching effectiveness seminars. They need to become convinced that academic grades should be separated from behavior grades. Unless teachers do this, there is much lacking in their performance. It is incumbent upon high school teachers to reward all students on the basis of their work. This holds true for classroom posters, written work, test performance, and related classroom activities.

Then, there were those students who rarely studied. For example, one former student was very intelligent, yet, he did not want to study his lesson. Instead, he liked to read and spent much of his time reading novels. It appears this student could have been encouraged to learn other things, especially, since he was a good reader. Then, there were those former students who went home after school, put their books down, and went out to play basketball and football. When night came they stood in the housing parks and talked and joked. One former student put it this way, " I played basketball and then hung out. That means, I joked with my friends and saw girls. Because I got home between ll and 12 p.m., there was no time to study. As a result, I did not do homework." Another student stated his situation thusly:

> My friends and I stayed up late at night. I partied all the time. There were girls at our parties. I partied because I was bored and

there was peer pressure. I didn't study because of poor study habits.

The problem, however, is twofold: black male high school students must learn to spend more time at home and receive the incentive to study. They must turn their backs on street life and the basketball and football arenas when it is time to study. The finding that a majority of the respondents did not have good study habits is a major key to dropping out. They needed to be taught before reaching high school to be well-disciplined in course preparation and performance and how to prepare classwork. If all African-American males become the best they can be in classroom achievement, many of the problems, including those with teachers and other students, will be alleviated. Besides, if teachers inspire their students to learn, there will be less classroom disturbance.

The bottom line is that all African-American recreational centers and African-American churches should have a strong nightly tutoring program. This business of not studying is critical to dropping out or being put out of high school. The challenge is for students to study and for the school, church, and recreational centers to assist. Of course, to get the momentum going, teachers must artistically create a classroom that is fair for all students and has an atmosphere for learning. This suggestion follows from the comments of the respondents that they do not like classes where ineffective teaching exists. Yet, African-Americans, regardless of classroom teaching style, must learn to learn as early as elementary school.

Teacher Harassment

The respondents also harassed their teachers. They talked back to their teachers and sometimes left the classroom to show their indignance. One former student said:"The teachers would say sit down and stop playing. In class, I was a clown and it made the students laugh. Yet, I knew when to be quiet." Similarly, according to another student, "I wanted attention like a movie star; as a result I disrupted the class to hold the students' attention more than the teacher." Other respondents talked about disrupting the class by talking, joking, and laughing. Indeed, this contributed to the difficulty of teaching an effective lesson.Interestingly, all these students were not making low grades. For example, one former student stated, "I talked a lot, laughed, and joked until the teacher said get quiet. I would be quiet for a little while and then I would start up again. My grades were mostly Bs and Cs." However, one of the most vivid cases among the former students was the student who reported:

I fought teachers and students. The teachers acted like they didn't like me. And I didn't study my lessons and do my homework but every two months.

Perhaps this student failed to do homework and caused disturbance because he perceived that the teacher did not like him. It is important for teachers to demonstrate to students a warm and caring attitude. A similar former student stated, "I was a bad hassle. They said that I had a bad reputation. They watched me and that offended me. They seemed to think that I was a trouble maker."

These cases suggest several factors, including the need for status and the need to be liked by one's teachers. The African-American male, as, Shawn Knight, a college freshman at The College of William and Mary, Williamsburg, Virginia and a respondent in the stayin study noted, needs to learn to get a "high" off achievement. This means they need help in refocusing their goals. Another implication of these findings is that when one student "acts up" in class, it disturbs the learning atmosphere for all students. Therefore, it is important to teach African-American high school males that class disruption not only hinders their learning but the entire educational process. In effect, there is a need to help the African-American male learn better self-control and be less dynamic in the classroom. Also, as Shawn Knight stated, "Before he acts, he should consider the consequences." It is urgent that this message gets deeply ingrained in the minds of young African-American males. The African-American males need adults to help make this occur; and teachers deserve an orderly classroom to maximize the learning process. A quick solution to teacher harassment should be forthcoming.

Dislike for School

We found that some dropouts disliked school. Because they were no longer in school was an indication that some types of behaviors caused them to drop out of high school. Five or six males explained that they got fed up with school and never liked it. One of these young men related, "I was having a lot of problems. It is like school was not for me. I could not really get there early. It wasn't for me. I wanted to do what I wanted to do. I was a knucklehead." Implicit in this respondent's statement is the possibility that he would have been in school if some adult could have made friends with him and helped him see why he would hurt himself by not listening to what is expected of young men--which is graduation from high school. Along the same line, at least one male left school because he needed to be pushed and no one was pushing him to get his lessons and stay in school.

Then, there was one respondent who could not stay in school. His mother had him to undergo psychiatric testing, but they could not find a problem. He would say, "Mom, I want to go back." He would return to school a couple of weeks and stop. It seemed that the more she pushed her son, the more he slacked off from school. He would attend the Norfolk Technical Vocational Center, but not high school. Then, a month before school ended, he stopped going to the Norfolk Technical Vocational Center. This young man needed someone to help him find himself and stay in school.

Their age also caused about fifteen of the respondents to dislike school. For example, when one respondent found out that he would be twenty one years old when he graduated, he decided to leave school. Another respondent, stated, "I dropped out of high school because of my age and I have no patience. And the teachers said that I was inattentive."

Respondents, Courses, Administrators and Teachers

This foursome also helped the respondents leave school before graduation (see Table 2-1).Starting with the respondents, we found that 5.7 percent dropped out of high school to rebel against one or both parents, 6.8 percent were too outgoing to be obedient, and 5.7 dropped out because they were confined. Most importantly, school was boring.

We turned from the respondents' behavior and boring schools to their school performance to determine whether it influenced them to drop out. This was an essential question because we believed if they had success in their classes and the principals' offices, they would be inspired to stay in school. Only 5.7 percent noted they dropped out of high school because they could not do their homework while 3.4 percent dropped out because they could not pass their tests. Even though they usually said they could do homework and pass tests, 19.3 percent indicated they had dropped out of high school because they earned mainly Ds and Fs. If, indeed, these students were capable, and we have no reason to disbelieve them, they needed assistance in getting them in the frame of mind to study and succeed.

Desiring to understand the classroom better, we asked whether they dropped out of school because they were not interested in the subjects they were taking. And, 22.7 percent noted this helped them to drop out of high school. It follows that 40.9 percent indicated that school was boring and contributed to them dropping out of high school.

Once we had seemingly pursued the dropouts' behavior, we asked them whether school officials contributed to them dropping out. We found that 9.1 percent dropped out of school because the principal made them angry while 19.3 percent said the assistant principal made them angry and therefore contributed to them dropping out of school. It appears that administrators should be trained to deal with all types of students and maintain a working relationship. If administrators cannot keep them calm, that poses a serious problem.

Next, we turned to the dropouts' former teachers. Realizing that most cases reach the principal through teachers, we asked the dropouts about

TABLE 2-1: Reasons African-American Males
Dropped Out of High School

Reasons for Dropping Out of High School	Percent
School was Boring	40.9
Disinterest in Subjects	22.7
Teacher Angered Student	20.5
Assist. Principal Angered Student	19.3
Low Grades (mostly Ds & Fs)	19.3
Required to be Quiet in Class	12.5
Insufficient Attention from Teachers	10.2
Principal Angered Student	9.1
Teacher Hurt Student's Feelings	9.1
Could not do Homework	5.7
Could not Pass Tests	3.4

their relationship with the teachers that contributed to their dropping out of school. We found that 20.5 percent noted that because a teacher or teachers angered them, it contributed to them dropping out of high school while 9.1 percent said that teachers hurt their feelings and, therefore, contributed to them dropping out of school. Interestingly enough, 10.2 percent noted that because teachers did not give them enough attention, it contributed to them dropping out. Even though they were males, they desired caring teachers.

Peer Pressure: Clothes, Hooking, and Hanging Out

Along with fighting,quick temper,poor study habits, teacher harassment, dislike for school, the respondents, their subjects, administrators, and teachers, there is another important problem, peer pressure. The former students

informed this study of varied adverse behavior they participated in because of peer pressure. One such type of behavior was missing or leaving
school because they did not have clothes like their friends. For example,
one respondent stated, "While I was in school, I did not have money to
buy clothes and shoes." The mother of a respondent described her son
thusly:

> He lost interest in school because he wasn't able to have money
> and clothing. His friends were drug dealers. They wore $100 tennis
> shoes.

As a dropout-transfer-returnee student stated, the African-American male
should learn to get an education and buy fine clothes and jewelry after he
gets an education. Indeed, this is a sound plan, however, the family, community, and school are needed to help not just a few, but a large number of
African-American high school males come to this realization.

Hooking was another type of behavior engaged in by the respondents
and their peers. One meaning of hooking is cutting classes. The respondents went to school and left before the end of the school day.
Occasionally, they returned to school before the day was over. In one
case, a former student and his friends left school and drank liquor during
lunchtime. Upon returning to school, a school offical smelled it on their
breath and they were suspended and later expelled. Also, hooking means
missing days out of school. The former students used that time for numerous activities. They went to the movies, used drugs, drank beer and liquor,
and engaged in sex. One respondent said that he was having a good time
with the girls, but it really was not fun. They went to the movies, engaged
in sex, and walked in the shopping malls. He concluded by saying that
even though school is not as much fun as hanging out, it is better to attend
school. Then, some of the dropouts played Nintendo or slept all day. Also,
on some days, while they were hooking, they fought gang wars or fought
members of their own gang. Unless they were drinking, usually they did
not fight gang members.

Hooking to hang out part or the entire day away from school was an
enormous problem for parents. The respondents often spent the day in
each other's homes. If parents did not work, the friendship group spent the
day in a house where the mother worked. And a majority of the time, the
respondents returned home at the end of the school day and a few arrived
late. Yet, they had good excuses and mothers were not suspicious that
their sons were hooking.

On the other hand, a few of the former students spent their hooking
days sleeping. When they did not have a key to the house, they returned
home and entered through the window and slept all day. Or, their mothers

went to work before it was time to leave home and they spent the day sleeping. On one occasion, one mother returned home to get something. She explains how she found out about her son missing days from school:

> I went out the door and came back in and found him in the clothes closet. He started crying. The problem was that he felt out of place with children younger than himself.And a couple of white teachers gave him problems. It was a racial thing.He wore an African-American tee shirt to school with certain positive wording about blackness. One white teacher told him that he could not wear it to school. He responded by saying that the tee shirt was about his father-land.Another white teacher asked,"Why do you act like a Nigger?" My son asked me to go to school and talk with the principal about this racial comment and tee shirt problem. I refused to go and told him the administration would not do anything about it.

When positive trends, such as tee shirts with enhancing messages about African-Americans, are in vogue, it would be a good idea for the administration to call in knowledgeable African-Americans and ask them to explain the trend to the faculty and student population. Education seems to be a sure way out of such dilemmas. And it appears that all high school administrators have the responsibility to make certain their teachers refrain from racial slurs. They are damaging to the self-concept of African-American males and, therefore, hinder their achievement--including staying in school-- and their sense of well-being in school.

As a rule, hooking was kept from the respondents' mothers until they were suspended, which was usually too late for the mothers to rescue their children. The former students intercepted the warning letters the schools sent their mother about their absenteeism or their mother was not at home when the electronic machine telephoned them in the evening to report the absenteeism of their children. In actuality, the mothers thought their sons were in school. Each morning some respondents awakened at the right time, got dressed, and left home. Technology is certainly useful in a large school population, but it needs to be more advanced. That is, the machine should be programmed to call various times of the day and night. It is not always definite that parents will be home at night. Mothers, as well as fathers, may very well have night jobs or recreational or religious activities. And it seems incumbent upon the school to make contact with parents. In yet another case, a mother did not have a telephone, was at home every day, and lived almost across the street from the school. She did not understand why someone from the school did not knock on her door--just once--to let her know that her son was not attending school. Also, the visiting teacher should give African-American males' absenteeism a personal touch by telephoning and visiting their parents. After missing school one day,

African-males should receive a care call or visit.

Some mothers never learned their children had been suspended. Thus when some of the respondents exceeded the fifteen days they were allotted to be absent, they continued in school, but did not pass to the next grade. Their mothers thought they were not doing their school work.

On the other hand, a few mothers of the respondents had secured mail boxes and received their children's warning and suspension letters; yet they were unsuccessful in keeping them in school. Parents should not be helpless when it comes to keeping their children in school. They should be taught early how to manage their children and schools should initiate other high standards. Moreover, schools should help students meet the standards. Parents, children, and the school should become a formidable team for preventing students from dropping out. Of course, one eighteen year old respondent wrote false excuses which were accepted in school. He said, "I wrote about six of them and they never caught up with me. And some days I went to school without a note." If males remain in school until they are eighteen years old, they should be given the same attention as younger students and not be allowed to miss days out of school.

Hanging out was another type of behavior. It occurred at night. The former students explained that they played ball, talked and laughed, and visited girls at night. When they got home it was late and, when morning came, they were too sleepy and tired to go to school on time. Hence, hanging out at night caused some respondents to be punished for arriving at school late. Then, there were other students who hung out on the way to school. Usually, they saw non-school friends and stopped and talked with them. When they got to school, they were meted out punishment.

There was another pattern of behavior among the former students that resembled hanging out in the streets. That pattern of behavior was hanging out at home. They watched television at home all night and were too sleepy to go to school the next morning or they arrived at school late.

It was not only hanging out in the streets or at home that mattered. It also included the type of persons with whom the respondents hung out. They hung out with young men who robbed, dealt drugs, fought, and enjoyed out of school behavior. According to a few of them, their groups were variously called, the wrong crowd, "hoodlums," or "mobs."

As we have shown, hanging out has enormous consequences for high school African-American males and should be a high priority in the school system, Sunday morning church messages, and civic programs. Hanging out at night and during the day as well as early morning ought to be halted immediately. The former students said that one way to do this is to make school more fun than hanging out. Certainly, it does challenge the school to energize their classrooms and assemblies. Also, African-American male potential putouts and dropouts need to be taught self-control; and hanging out, during school and study time, should be changed. The approach should include the school, church, and community. The concept hanging out, as described by the respondents, is a pattern of behavior that needs to be deleted from the lives of African-American males.

Expensive clothes and shoes, hooking, hanging out, and intercepting messages from schools are real problems that require families to see that their homes are never available for hooking, business establishments in the community to make their locations unavailable for hooking, and schools to devise a method that allows parents, especially the mother, to have at least one personal contact about her child's problem before it is too late. When approaching these major problems, it is important to remember that many students hook and hang out because of peer pressure. Hence, African-American males, across the board, should be taught not to hook and hang out; further, African-American males need to have instilled in them an aggressive drive for learning, diplomas, and degrees, and discontent with peers who seek to interfere with these goals.

Multiple Problems

A majority of the students experienced one or more of the problems described. To indicate the variety of problems that an individual student experienced, two cases will be analyzed. Our first respondent's multiple problems were created mainly by himself. He told us:

> I dropped out of high school because I did not have the right clothes to wear. Also, I missed a lot of days out of school. Added to this, I was lazy. What I mean by this,is that I had a problem getting up in the morning because I went to bed too late. I stayed up watching television or playing Nintendo until about 2 a. m. or 3 a. m. in the morning.

Peer pressure is a far reaching behavior among the respondents. It surfaces in many areas of their lives. In this case, it was clothes and staying up late at night, which caused him to miss school the next day.

The second respondent stated:

> I dropped out of high school because I was having problems with students and teachers. The bullies were fighting me over things like a sheet of paper, pencils, and stuff. They would say things like "I'll see you after school." Then,there were the teachers. They acted like they didn't want to teach. They didn't explain the work

or anything.I would say Mr. or Miss (So and So) I don't know how to do this assignment.The response was,"Well, do it and I'll tell you if you get it right." I said something like, I'll just do it this way. The teachers took this as a smart remark and responded, "Well, since you know so much, tell the class. (The student was embarrassed because he did not know how to carry out the teacher's request).

This student also had difficult problems with his peers. That is, he was threatened by them and perhaps anticipated all day what it would be like after school. Piled on top of this, the student did not understand the school work and when help was sought, he did not receive help nor a good feeling about himself. Another finding that emerged from this respondent's multiple problems is something that surfaced early in our research; that is, African-American males need to hear school work explained in terms they can understand and in great depth. Besides, they need to see teachers draw models of their work on the chalkboard, write notes on the chalkboard, and engage the class in critical thinking exercises to help African-American males learn to think through assignments. And, by all means, when a student asks for help the teacher should caringly give it.

African-American males need help with their personal behavior, such as the need to go to school daily and to bed early. Therefore, the Norfolk African-American male dropouts had multiple problems that required multiple solutions. These findings and others in this chapter indicate that some African-American parents, especially mothers, cannot control their sons. Hence, African-American parents need the African-American community to teach their sons to be obedient and adults to be good parents. This kind of grassroots training will help young African-American males overcome their personal dilemmas.

Chapter 3   Structural Factors That Contributed to Dropping Out of
            School

The African-American male high school dropouts not only put themselves at risk, but organizations also put them at risk of leaving school. For
example, there were structural factors in the school, criminal justice system,
and family that caused African-American males to drop out of high school.
Some structural factors in school were racism, student harassment, and
teacher behavior. Also, help with homework and greater opportunities
were needed. Further, suspensions, school hearings, and expulsions
caused the respondents to drop out of high school. Besides, when they
ran afoul of the law, the criminal justice system interfered with their schooling. Similarly, parental problems and interpersonal relations with parents
caused a few African-American males to leave school. Hence, dropping out
of school is a complex phenomenon linked to major patterns of behavior.

Racism

As indicated in Chapter 2, racism (unequal treatment of the races) exist-
ed in the Norfolk Public High Schools. The high school male dropouts
faced racism in all school settings. For example, it was encountered with
their white counselors. Counselors should be the best school friend that a
student has. Yet, their offices are part of the problem of the collective
African-American male student. For example, one former high school student explained his encounter with racism in the counseling office thusly:

> Before I got kicked out,I was trying to get in the Pass Program. It
> allows one to pass in a semester.My counselor explained a little
> about it.Football boys were in the Pass program and had tutors,
> but they would not give it to me. I filled out three applications, but
> my counselor never called me back. I really wanted to talk with
> my white counselor. After a while, I forgot about her. If I got be-
> hind in my school work, I didn't bother to go see her.

Indeed, the student was positively aggressive in trying to get into the Pass
Program, but his counselor was non-responsive. When the student was
not given the opportunity to talk with her the way he wanted, he gave up
on the counseling department and missed graduation from high school.
Let it be noted that this research report does not suggest there should be
no cross-racial counseling. If anything, this report encourages it, because,
as will be shown in this chapter, Black administrators and teachers, as well
as their white counterparts, were viewed as giving unfair treatment. Hence,
the suggestion here is that counseling departments in high schools have
the responsibility to effectively assist all students with their problems.

The former students also faced racism with their white peers. In one case, it occurred in study hall. One respondent stated:

> I did something wrong, but the teacher did not see me. She took the student's word. It was a white female student who told on me. And she and I never really got along. We were at each other's throat.What happened is that Blacks sat together on one side of the room and whites sat together on the other side of study hall. The Blacks made racial comments about whites and whites did the same for Blacks. You could sense the tension in study hall.The difference is that we said our comments loud and the white students whispered their comments and laughed. When a problem was carried to the Black and white administrators, they listened to the white students more than to us.

This study hall had an adversarial atmosphere that was not geared to studying. Instead, it was characterized by bullying more so than preparation of school work. Racial tension between white and African-American students should be alleviated. This should be a top priority. It will contribute to a "kinder" high school, community, and probably enhance the control that African-American male students have over the school environment. Also, it will enrich the entire school. Without control of their school setting, African-American males cannot realize their full potential in school life.

The respondents also experienced racism involving white students and white administrators. One of the most vivid cases appears below. This respondent stated:

> I was suspended three times. Once I was suspended because I fought about white racism. A white male student called me "Nigger." I hit him. I fought him. What happened is that I bumped into him turning a corner in a hall at school. I hit him real hard. It hurt him. He said, "Nigger," you better watch where you are going." When I heard that, I punched him four or five times. He was swinging back, but missed each time. My friend said chill out and pulled me off him.

> The next day, a white girl told the principal that we were fighting. And a Black girl volunteered my name. They called me to the office and gave me a five day suspension. They didn't do anything to the white student who called me "Nigger." The white assistant principal told me that "Nigger" is a figure of speech and that I had to take it like a man. However, if anybody calls me "Nigger", I will take action. White folks aren't suppose to say this. We have passed this stage.

In this case, it is clear that a white male high school administrator allowed a white male student to call an African-American male student a demeaning name. What immediately emerges out of this case, as in similar cases, is that disciplinary principals and officers need to be specially and continually trained for what is probably the most important position in the school. Furthermore, the African-American male had to contend with a white female, an African-American female, and a white male as well as an uncaring administrator.

Perhaps an equally vivid case of racism experienced by the respondents involved only the school administration and a counselor. The former student, in this case, reported as follows:

> I brought a walk-man and ear phones to school. A teacher and I didn't get along; he snatched them. They weren't mine. I asked when could I get them? He said they would be returned at the end of the semester. Since they weren't mine, I took them off his desk. He sent a referral to the office. Without letting me talk in the office, they suspended me five days. When I returned to school the white principal told me I couldn't pass. I asked for a change of schedule. The white principal and white guidance counsellor said they couldn't change my schedule. A white guy, right in my face, got his schedule changed. I said, you changed his schedule, why not mine? Then I asked, Where did he get his schedule changed? They said he came to us. I answered, I came to you. If the principal had changed my schedule, I would have graduated.

This example can be no more than blatant racism levied by professional adults against an African-American male. Moreover, it appears that the administration needs to find how to say "You can pass," instead of " You cannot pass." Also, apparently, administrators use the expression, "You cannot pass," as a weapon against misbehaving African-American males. They seem to feel that once the student learns he cannot pass, the troublemaker will leave school. African-American males need to know this and make trouble run from them. This can be more easily achieved when the school becomes a more concerned institution about the African-American male.

Moreover, when a teacher sends a referral note to the office, the entire case needs to be investigated to make a decision. For example, the teacher who referred this respondent to the office was personally involved with the student in another classroom situation. According to the respondent, this particular teacher was always on his back and hurt his feelings. This was evident when he asked for help with his homework. Instead of helping him, the teacher was sarcastic. He said, "You can be smart with your friends and now you need my help?"   After the teacher finished speaking, according to the respondent, "Everybody in the class laughed."

According to this former student, he often asked the teacher to stay after school and help him with his school work, but he always said that he was leaving at 2:30. However, on certain days, he would stay at school to punish the former student. When this occurred, they stayed at school until 4 p. m. Instead of helping him with his lesson, he required the student to straighten desks, sweep the floor, and wash the chalkboards. The former student also reported that this same teacher talked to him in an adversarial manner. For example, he told the student that he didn't have manners and that he knew for sure that he would be locked up in prison within the next six to twelve months. This case essentially abolishes African-American manhood and aspirations. Instead of helping the student obtain his full potential, the teacher predicted dire circumstances. What we must understand is that, like everyone else, high school African-American males have feelings and desire success. This student certainly had feelings and was hurt by the teacher's perspective. To add to the student's discouragment, he was punished by being required to do janitorial duties and serving as the butt of classroom jokes. When this case is put in total perspective, open racial inequality is paraded in front of the student. What of him? He was helpless and battered around by students (laughs), a teacher, and administrators.

The dropouts also wanted to be listened to. According to them, when they went to the office, frequently the disciplinary administrators and the hearing committee either did not allow African-American males to tell their perspective or abbreviated it. The concern here is for African-American and white teachers, counselors, and white and African-American administrators to let African-American male students tell their side of the story and assess it with the same sincerity as they assess any other student's case. According to one respondent, there is a standard response African-American administrators make toward an African-American student who is sent to the office for misbehavior. They take him into the office and say, "You knew better." The respondents saw this as a cop out. The African-American administrator seemed to have been giving an excuse for the punishment he was about to mete out to the respondent. In fact, how did the administrator know that he knew better. And if the student knew better, he did not act better and obviously was in need of better training; and the African-American administrator placed the blame on the victim.

Student Harassment

Racism is indeed harassment, however, the dropouts and putouts identified other forms of harassment from African-American and white teachers. According to the former students, it took varied forms. For example, it was seen in the language teachers used with students. To illustrate, one former student was suppose to be in a certain class. Instead, he was talking with a friend in a different class. The white teacher told him: "Get out of here before I kick your butt." And there was an exchange of words. Not only was the student the recipient of unprofessional communication, but he received a fifteen day suspension and never returned to school. In another case, when a respondent acted up in class, because he was age nineteen and in the ninth grade, the African-American teacher embarrassed him by the way she said it. He did not mind her using him as an example to help other students, but he desired her to say it in a concerned way.

Teachers also harassed students when they suspected them of dealing in drugs. For example, an African-American teacher called one of the respondents to the side and told him that he was a drug dealer and drove around in the area where he lived. This was his metal shop teacher. The teacher told him that he had an attitude and talked with him about his attitude. The former student got smart. Then, the teacher told him to stand in the hall and cool off. The respondent said, " I felt that it was none of his business what I did after school, on the streets, or during the summer." The former student left school after three weeks into the semester.

In another case, a coach harassed a student when he stopped playing football. A former student reported on his relationship with his former football coach as follows:

> I was a freshman and played football. When I got in fights, Mama told me to stop playing football. Subsequently, every time the football coach saw me, he picked on me. He would ask, "Where are you going?" While I played football, everything was alright. The coach is a hall monitor. He stopped my girlfriend and myself around 8:30 one morning. He asked me, "Where are you going?" I told him that I was going to my first bell class. He responded, " You are not going to be here the whole year. I'm going to make sure of that. I said, If that's the way you feel about it, do it. He smiled. And I went to my class. That made me feel that he was out to get me.

This former student was caught between his mother's decision and the coach's desire for him to play football. Can we expect that this student was able to concentrate on his school work that day and the remainder of the days he went to school? The student continued thusly:

> If the coach heard my name on the walkie-talkie, he would go to the office and look and see which principal's office I was in and leave. If they called my name on the intercom, he would do the same. This was a Black coach. The assistant principal was white.

> Sometimes when I went to the office, the coach said, "We got him
> now. You are gone now." I would always ask, Why you don't like
> me or why are you out to get me? He would just smile.

This African-American coach treated the respondent like a criminal rather
than like a student. Is there an administrative authoritarian mentality monitoring the halls in our schools and coaching our high school football
teams? Can this type of behavior be ignored? The answer is no if we are
serious about maintaining African-American males in high school and helping them graduate.

In still another case, a dropout reported that a white teacher harassed
him. The student was spinning a ruler with a pencil. The respondent reported the case thusly:

> The white male teacher said, "Put that stick down."I told him that it
> was a ruler. He took my ruler and said that I would not get it back
> until June. I cuffed and grabbed the white male teacher and he
> wrote a referral note to the office.

This example of student harassment and extensive punishment over a simple act of spinning a ruler enraged the student and caused him to misbehave and get suspended. This case seems to reinforce the need to enhance
the self-image of some teachers. The severity of the punishment seems
out of line with the act. And it appears that punishment should fit the act;
or give the student the benefit of the doubt. Also, it is important that administrators and teachers refrain from creating rage in African-American
males. It is only an excuse to get rid of them. Community leaders and
well-meaning teachers of all races ought to tell African-American males
that when administrators and teachers create rage in them it is a means of
depriving them of an education. When young males learn the reality of the
situation, they can refuse behavior that results in missing a high school education.

In still another case, one respondent was bending down on the floor
playing with a pencil. His physical education teacher kicked the pencil
and after he responded unkindly, the teacher, he says, picked him up by his
pants and threw him out. He returned to school later, but things were not
the same and he just drifted away. What seems to have been missing in the
interpersonal relations between teachers and students is the recognition
that these respondents are human beings and young men who should
have been treated as young adults.

In some other cases, students became frustrated over school work. One
former student noted that he could do the school work, but the teachers

were saying that he could not do It. He said that when he passed in his homework, he had checked it twice. According to him, his work was right, but two of his white teachers said that it was wrong. He indicated that one was racist and suspended him from study hall and got him suspended from school for allegedly making noise. The former student said, that "Instead of making noise, I was trying to go to sleep. I went to sleep." To have an effective school, it is not fair to punish students in one situation because of a previous adverse experience. Yet this finding surfaced more than once in the data. Rather than being warm and caring teachers, some of them engaged in warfare with a youthful population that needed an education.

Teachers also harassed students through mistaken identity. A case in point follows. A respondent reported:

> One teacher said that I cursed her. I said that is a bunch of bull....
> We were in the in-school detention. She said be quiet. Somebody said something and she thought that it was me. She said that my time would start over because I was making noise. I then said, that it was a bunch of bull. She wrote a referral note. I went home after she wrote the referral note to the office. The next day they called me to the office and suspended me two days.

This case has the appearance of a faulty legal situation outside a school room. The former student was mistakenly accused and his time in detention was extended. Moreover, the mistaken identity episode created rage in the former student.

Rage was also evident in this case. A former student said:

> My teachers made me angry. They picked on me. There would be thirteen or twenty students in a class, but the teachers would ask me the questions. I was getting tired of it. I wasn't a talkative person. This all happened in my math and physical education classes. And the teachers always told the class that I was a bad example in the classroom and the students laughed.

The former students clearly demonstrate that teachers help create rage in African-American male high school students. And it is somewhat widespread. When rage is created or brought to the surface, it is unlikely that the students will perform in the classroom. African-American males should be taught this is the case and to fight back. It is time for the African-American males to fight back consistently. They should tactfully tell their adult white and African-American accusers that they suspect racism in their decisions and request an end to it. And, by all means, teach them not to fight back with verbal or physical violence.

Indeed teacher harassment took many forms among the former high school students. They included unprofessional language and voice tone, anger, unfair grading, telling students they couldn't do the work, mistaken identity in punishment, prediction of imprisonment, prediction of expulsion from school, "picking on them," and failure to listen to what they had to say. For whatever reasons, teacher harassment is bound to have an ad-verse effect on students' attitudes, school attendance, and performance. Weekly workshops during faculty meetings would call teachers' attention to what they are doing to African-American males and help them to take a positive and helpful approach toward them.

Teaching

A majority of the respondents informed this study that, in general, the Norfolk Public School System has good teachers. However, a few ineffec-tive teachers caused the dropouts to lose interest in school. Also, they pointed to particular problems in the teaching arena. They considered tak-ing test part of the teaching process and, in their opinion, teachers did not measure up to their needs. For example, often they did not know the meaning of the words on the test and found it hard to understand why the teachers would not define the words in simpler language to enable them to answer the questions. In cases of this type, there is plenty of room for in-terdisciplinary teaching or teaching vocabulary across the curriculum. African-American male high school students should have a vocabulary that matches the level of their tests.

They had yet a different type of problem. They experienced teachers who didn't teach the "facts of the course." For example, one former stu-dent described his algebra teacher:

> He didn't teach the facts of algebra. He was like a commedian. That is, he told jokes about things that happened in his home and on television shows. And always asked whether we had seen the Cosby show. When we said yes, he asked questions about it. We didn't get much algebra because the bell soon rang.

Another problem the former students experienced was boring teachers. When asked to describe these teachers, the respondents related varied ways the teachers were considered boring. For example, they stated that some teachers gave long lectures and ended the week with tests. Perhaps the most boring teacher described was a science teacher. He lectured and a few students took notes, but most students found the course too diffi-cult. A respondent, in discussing this class said, "The course was not a bit interesting. I didn't get any help. This one class pulled me down. I worried so much about it until I forgot my other subjects For two weeks, at a time, the biology teacher lectured and then gave a test. We had to listen to him and take notes and he only wrote a little on the board." This teacher needed to participate in a seminar on teaching high school students. When students do not learn what they teach, teachers need to teach the way students learn.

In describing his boredom, another former student indicated that he went to sleep in class and said, "I can't sit in a class forty five minutes doing nothing except reading a book. In my English class, we were required to read a book the entire bell and I would fall asleep."

In a similar case, a student did not go to school in the mornings because his English class was boring. He said they used the textbook *World Adventure*. According to him, his female teacher did not teach the class. Instead, they silently read, in class, the whole book. For example, two days, each week, he said, they read silently the whole bell. The next day the teacher gave them questions on the book; and the following day she gave them the answers. The last day of the week she gave a test. He concluded by saying, "The teacher did not even review what we had read and I went to sleep a lot." This student seems to be suggesting the need for the state of the art teaching in high school literature. Indeed, there is much latitude for making literature an interesting class therefore the student was not suggesting an impossible course of action.

Similarly, a former student explained that "Some days the teachers only wrote information on the board." Yet, this same student said, "If I missed a day, some teachers would help me catch up by giving me take home assignments." In effect, there were more good than poor teachers in this public school system, but it only takes a few ineffective teachers to cause some African-American males to lose interest in school.

Another respondent was even more analytical and described his boredom this way:

> School was boring because they were not teaching me what I needed to know. They were not teaching what will help me in the real world. They were not teaching what Blacks need to know. For example, why do we need to know about the Japanese and don't know anything about ourselves. We need real changes in history. There is nothing in it for Blacks. They teach us about whites. We learn about whites. Whites also need to know something about us--other than slavery.

This former student was bored in history class because it did not meet two basic needs: how to manage the real world and, slavery excepted, knowledge about the background of African-Americans. Indeed, all students deserve teachers who teach meaningful lessons and about the outstanding contributions of African-Americans.

Another respondent gave an adverse view of teaching in his high school:

> Teachers aren't in to teaching. They will not help you with your school work, they get an attitude, and blame students for not learning. The majority of the classes in my school are overcrowded. And some teachers know the material and some don't. Then, there are those teachers who try to move too fast for the students. I had no academic problems, however, I only studied when needed and that was for tests. So, actually, I studied occasionally. As you can imagine, my grades went up and down.

To keep other students from wasting or being caused to waste their intellect, we asked how teachers could make their classes more exciting. In response, one former student described his English teacher. He said, " "English was appealing. The teacher had a relationship with our class. She had variety in teaching. We discussed stories, read novels, and discussed them. I like reading. I take time out to read. And she asked us questions about the lessons." Some other former students responded by saying that teachers should have humor, which would make them more interesting and fun to be with as well as great to talk with.

One former student remarked, "I am a quiet one. If my teachers had been different, I would have stayed in school. They should joke along and have a nice tone of voice. Also, when making assignments, they should be pleasant. In other words, the way teachers look at students reflects back to the students. Frowns on their face brought frowns on my face." Another thing this former student related is that "The way teachers present themselves at the beginning of the term tells how the classes will go. If they look difficult, there will be hard class sessions." Then, he described a particular teacher thusly:

> I had one teacher who came into the classroom and seemed to ask, without saying it, why we were there. We knew the class would not be normal. Nobody asked to go to the restroom and there were no questions. Nobody raised his or her hand. We sat with our heads in our hands. She became angry and we did not respond.

Strong teaching and a pleasant and caring disposition are important ways to make high school classes interesting.

According to another respondent, an important problem is that "Teachers don't teach what is on the test. The material has to be studied." If, indeed this is the case, it seems reasonable for teachers to at least teach what is on the test even if they do not test on all they teach.

Also, the respondents noted that orderly classes would have made them more interesting. A lack of order in some classrooms caused some students to fail to see the importance of school. As one student put it, "Classrooms were noisy. Students joked, played, acted crazy, read magazines, and wrote on the board. The teachers watched and laughed. Some of the teachers joked with students and we would not get much lesson done that bell." These findings suggest that a few teachers, as well as students, are responsible for boring classes. Some students have a high tolerance level for boring classes while they caused other students to perform poorly or leave school. That is, boring classes do not motivate some students. According to the respondents, some African-American males often were not motivated in high school. For example, one stated, "I wasn't doing anything constructive in high school. I was wasting my time and wasn't interested or motivated to do my school work or participate in school activities." This type of student needs a great deal of help to get him into the school mode. And it appears this responsibility rests mainly with the school. Why? Because they are trained as teachers while many fathers and mothers are unaware of effective motivation techniques.

Needed Help With Homework

Some respondents did not study because they did not know how to do their homework. A few teachers helped them, but they did not get nearly as much help as they needed. Some of the former students seemed to have been desperate for teacher help. For example, a respondent stated, "The teachers should have helped me with my lessons. Other teachers could have started helping me with my behavior in the eighth grade." Even though the former students appeared intellectually capable, it was also evident that they needed more teacher help after school. They even mentioned that teachers were ready to leave at the close of the school day; and that was the time they would have appreciated personal assistance. When one student did not know how to do his work, it was easy for peer pressure to influence him. For example, he said, "Sometimes I didn't know how to do the school work or I didn't feel like it. My friends encouraged me to go with them to the movies. I made all Es (failing grades) and that was discouraging. I like fun and attention." Because some of them did not know how to do their homework, they substituted fun, attention, movies, basketball, football, and partying for studying. Hence, it is clear that even though the respondents appeared to have good intellect, there were some respondents who needed help. And as they look back, they wish the teachers had helped them not only with their lessons but also with their behavior.

Greater Opportunities Needed

Some of the former students had the need for greater opportunities. For example, one of them tried to get his schedule changed to take a computer course. The results of his efforts were that it was too late to get a schedule change and that he must stay in study hall. There were other former students who wanted to learn a trade at the only public school technical vocational center in Norfolk and were denied because of the limitation on enrollment. One former student stated his situation this way:

> Things happened at school that also contributed to me becoming a dropout. While in school, I wanted to participate in the program at the Norfolk Technical Vocational Center. I signed up for woodwork. That was my first choice. We had to make a second choice. I just wrote food service, but I really wanted woodwork. I was assigned food service. In this class, we mainly sat around and that made the class boring. When we cooked, I didn't enjoy it. If I could have gotten into the woodwork class, which I like, that would have encouraged me to stay in school.

There are several obvious messages in this former student's comments. First, school systems need to provide for the needs of African-American males. Since there are some who are good with their hands, they need the opportunity to learn how to put them to use. It appears that if African-American males were allowed to follow their school career interests, such as computing and vocations, they would stay in school in larger numbers.

Academically Gifted and Talented Classes Unknown to Most African-American Students

Another way to make school interesting is to make known to all students, at the beginning of their stay in a particular school, complete information about the academically gifted and talented classes. This will give them more goals and incentives to do their school work.

One of the respondents dropped out of school because he was put into talented and gifted classes that were almost totally white and a majority of African-American students had not heard about them. The respondent reported his story of dropping out this way:

> I left school in the tenth grade because of my Designated Gifted and Talented courses. My white counselor suggested that I take the courses and warned they would be difficult. I took history, sci-

ence, and algebra for the gifted and put too much on myself. I thought that I could manage and hang in there. In these classes, they don't check homework. As a result, I slacked up because I knew they weren't checking papers. Finally, I dropped science and kept history and algebra.

When I was enrolled in all three gifted classes, I did a little science, read history, and studied algebra. If the teachers had said read hard, I would have done so. Since they didn't, I mostly looked and glanced over the work. I didn't know we would have so many pages on the test. I could have managed, but I am not the kind of person who could stay in the house studying hours and hours every page in all my books and learning every detail. I skimmed and read a couple of pages. In history, I read almost everything. I didn't read science very much, but I kept trying to catch up with the other students.

My grades fell. I received E in science, D in history, and C in algebra. I was set back, because I was expecting to graduate without an E. I dropped out of school because of these grades. I kept thinking about my grades.

If there had been more Blacks in the classes, that would have made me do better. There were only two or three other Blacks in the classes. It made me feel uncomfortable.

Another thing, when I talked about my gifted and talented classes, I learned that most Blacks at school had never heard about these classes. If there had been an equal number of Blacks and whites, I would have made it. I didn't feel too good around those people. The teachers were even white. Actually, there were only two other Blacks in my classes. They, too, must have felt strange. The people at my school probably didn't tell Blacks about the courses because they thought they were stupid.

I got along with whites in the classes, but we weren't friends who could visit and see each other after school.

This experience caused me to switch roles. I related to whites in my class on their terms and to my Black friends on their terms. That is, when I was with my Black friends I tried to be hip. I couldn't meet a good friend in the classes. Everybody kept to themselves. I didn't feel like family in those classes. I felt they didn't want me in there because I knew about racism and I am sure they knew about it. When we discussed slavery, in my history class, sometimes white students laughed. I didn't see anything funny. They probably thought they were better than the three of us--they had the upper hand. I wish the races had been equal. I felt they didn't want me to make it. I felt that some of the students were prejudiced. Some of them didn't associate with me. I didn't think anybody cared about me. I couldn't go over to their house and study. I was thinking about asking the advance teachers to tutor me, but I didn't.

Between the 1988-89 school term I had to go to court. When I went to school the fall of 1989, I couldn't concentrate. Mama didn't tell me what it would be like if I dropped out of school. I have to go through something. Now, I prefer to have gone through school. I plan to get my GED. When I returned to school in September, 1989, I stayed a short while. I had something to drink and was sent to the office and got suspended.

This case tells a great deal about a high school and African-American males. First, according to the respondent, almost all of them had never heard of classes in the school for the gifted and talented. Had they known, perhaps more would have worked hard to get in them. It seems incumbent upon each individual school to educate all students about the total curriculum and its requirements. Second, because of the imbalance of the races, the young respondent felt uncomfortable. This suggests that he did not have control over his classroom environment and would not do as well as he could have. Third, although he clearly delineates what was needed in the courses, the respondent suggests that he was not disciplined. Fourth, African-American males need a structured learning experience. It is important for teachers to correct their homework, make suggestions and comments, and return it to them. African-American males tend to get lost in an unstructured situation. Fifth, the respondent knew about racism and felt that he was not wanted. A sense of being unwanted would also impact his grades. Sixth, at the end of the classes, his gifted and talented peers did not study with him. He did not feel a part of the gifted classes. Seventh, the respondent suggests the need for a good mix in classes, including the gifted and talented. Certainly, it is critical that young capable African-American males be kept in high school and in the advance programs. And the less capable African-American males should be kept in school and helped to graduate. Indeed, the respondent, in this case, was able to be an excellent high school student and bemoans the fact that his mother did not explain how hard life is outside high school. And regrets the racial imbalance in the gifted and talented classes. It appears that the problems that the respondent faced in the gifted classes can be eliminated by family and teachers helping African-American males to make better grades. This could very well include personal tutoring.

Harassment from In-School Security Guards

A few of the former students informed this study that they were harassed by the security guard in their school. A case in point is a student who returned after a four month suspension. For three or four weeks, the security guard harassed him. He checked his trousers, emptied his pockets and coats, and lifted the legs of his trousers. According to several students, the security guards "pick at you and try to embarass you by saying bad things like you got suspended. Security guards get on your nerves. They pick at you and call you trifling."

Suspensions

When African-American males engaged in the behavior described in this book, it usually meant dropping out or being put out of high school. Suspensions were among the foremost reasons for African-American male students discontinuing their public school education. The school law is that if one misses more than fifteen days out of school, the student is dropped from the roll. Yet the suspensions among the respondents were epidemic. The former students in our study had received too many suspensions for them to remember the exact number. Therefore, they gave us approximate numbers. Not only were suspensions repetitive in the lives of the young men, but they were extensive. They ranged from two days to an entire semester. Suspensions are a clear signal that an African-American male is a potential dropout and should be helped immediately. While suspended, he needs special attention with his school work, school problems, and social relations with his friends and schoolmates.

While learning that suspensions were characteristically an experience of the respondents, we asked why they were suspended. Their suspension letters resulted from varied types of behavior, including tardiness. For example, one student was suspended for being late three days. After that he only remained in school two or three months. The former students did not believe that a student should be given out of school suspensions for repeated tardiness.

Another reason for suspensions was hooking after going to school. Some of them missed classes, such as health, mathematics, and study hall; or, they left at lunch time and did not return. One former student missed study hall everyday and felt there should be no punishment for missing it. His rationale was that, although there were teachers present, no one studied. Then, he informed this research that, if everybody had studied, he still would have missed it because he had drug using friends in study hall. That is the same reason he gave for missing algebra, his last class in the school day.   This suggests the long arm of drugs.   Not only do they impact the users, but they hinder friends of users from attending classes and graduating from high school.   Hence, the impact of drugs extends beyond the users and dealers.

Still another reason some of the African-American high school males got suspended was because they ate at the wrong lunch period.   One former student who got suspended for this reason explained:

> I have been suspended two or three times. One suspension was received because I ate at the first instead of the second lunch period to be with my friends.

The security guard took him to the office for eating at the wrong lunch period.   Because he had missed a lot of days from school, the disciplinary officer gave him a bus ticket home.   Since the former student had missed more than fifteen days, he decided to drop out of high school.

Frequently, the former students got suspended for fighting. For example, one of the former students got a twenty day suspension for fighting another African-American male.   He fought his fellow student because he stole his gym shorts and would not give them back.   According to the former student, he could see his shorts on the student's body.   When he wouldn't take them off, he beat him.   The respondent said, "People don't think I can fight.   I just know how to hit.   My friends and uncles taught me how to hit.   I am short and people doubt my fighting ability.   I am a Jack in the Box.   They get a surprise when they fight me."   This case suggests the need for African-American males to develop greater self-control and find alternative ways of resolving their problems.   In fact, they should be taught that peaceful solutions outweigh violence.   When this is understood, they will be less likely to take disciplining into their own hands.

According to another respondent:

> I got in a fight because a guy slapped my sister and left his hand print on her face. The second time we fought, the other guy got suspended and I got detention. I'd rather be in detention than suspended because suspension goes on your record. I think that suspension works for some people, but not for everybody. Some people change, but others don't. Most people on suspension run the streets. My aunt made me study while I was on suspension. I had a C average; and before I started going to high school, I had a B average.   Hanging around with the wrong people and cutting classes brought my average down.

Indeed, this respondent makes a noteworthy point when he indicates that suspensions are useful in some cases and unfruitful in others. The insightful administrator would take time to determine the effectiveness of particular types of punishment on each student. Foremost, the goal should be to improve the student's behavior and help him graduate from high school.

Another respondent got expelled two months for fighting a white male student. The former student reported:

> While we were walking down the hall, he bumped me. I asked, Can you say excuse me? He responded, "No, I can't say excuse me." Two friends helped me beat him. That's why I got expelled two months.

> After I fought him that day, the school officials consistenly checked my locker and my girlfriend's locker for weapons, but they never checked the white boy's locker. He didn't get expelled; he only got a two day suspension.

> I went back to school, stayed there four months, began hating it, and wanted to transfer. It was difficult to get a transfer, so I dropped out of high school.

This student needed some assistance in fighting back. He did not initiate the violence. At first, the violence was physical and was not begun by the African-American student. Why can't white males be taught to be polite to African-American males? In this case, it would have extended if not saved the high school career of an African-American male. Because his self-esteem was hurt, the African-American male began to hate school that held the key to the remainder of his life. Administrators, teachers, counselors, and security guards should be careful not to turn African-American males' attention away from school. It is their duty to make certain that each student has the type of daily experience that will make him stay in school.

Some other students were suspended because of teacher-student problems. According to one former student, "School is depressing. It does not hear both sides of a situation. When the school does not hear both sides, it makes the student think the school is taking sides with the teacher. Also, we have some rude African-American teachers." It appears that all African-American students should report a good experience with teachers of their own race. African-American teachers should be sympathetic, excellent, helpful, and warm and caring toward African-American males as well as toward all other students. Moreover, administrators need to get out of the mode of upholding teachers' behavior in the presence of students. It appears that they should be fair to the teachers and students and indeed there are some teachers who provoke disciplinary situations. Hence, often there is no reason to take sides with the teacher. The bottom line should be to support the person who is not initially at fault.

There were other reasons that explain suspensions. For example, one former student was in a restaurant near the school when the security guard and assistant principal raided it. They suspended him and the other students three or four days.

Whiskey on their breath was another reason for some suspensions. On the other hand, one respondent was involved with alcohol and the school helped him and he will return to school, graduate, and enter Norfolk State University. He told his suspension story this way:

> I had a bottle of alcohol at one of our basketball games. A principal saw it. Before I got in the stadium, they checked my jacket because I was acting suspicious and strange. My knees were hurting and I was not walking straight. But the main reason they searched me is that I had on a big jacket and I had loud behavior because I had a drink before I got to the game. They did not let me go into the stadium; instead, they took me into a classroom. The principal said, in the room, that I was suspended indefinitely. They actually suspended me four weeks. Then, I had a hearing. After the hearing, they sent me to the Chemical Abuse Prevention Through Education Services (CAPES). They taught us the facts of different drugs and how to deal with them. I went to CAPES two hours a day and worked on a job the rest of the day. At the end of CAPES, the last two weeks were automatically excused.

In this student's situation, the school helped him and allowed him to return to school. He appeared pleased with the consideration and assistance the school gave him and he straightened out his school life for a while.

Still another dropout got suspended for having beepers in his locker. He would not give the beepers to the disciplinary officer. Actually, the former student said, the beepers were in somebody else's locker, but he was standing near that locker. Consequently, they suspended him ten days.

A case of mistaken identity explains more vividly how easy it was for African-American males to get suspended in high school. This former student gave the following report:

> Someone reported to the school office that they saw me riding in a teacher's car, however, somebody else took the car. The day it occurred, they called me to the office and told me they were going to suspend me. I was not going to leave until they talked with Mom. They were wrong and still are wrong. I was in all my classes all

day long the day the car was taken. Yet, they suspended me ten days for supposedly riding in the car. The Black assistant principal got on my nerves. He kept pushing me to say that I did it. I said, to him, I told you what I had to say. They later found the car in Washington, D. C. and did not find out who took the car. The only one out of luck was me. I had no problems with my classes. It was about 1 p.m. when they said they saw me riding in the car. Perhaps my light skin color and box fade hair cut had something to do with them suspending me. During the ten day suspension, someone came forth and said that I was in all my classes. Mama became upset and said that I could not make up the work that I had missed during the ten days. Mama wanted me to attend another school. It took a month to get a transfer. The assistant principal apologized for the transfer delay; and a school official told an appropriate officer in the school board office that they believed they were wrong and that I was right.

If they had not made the mistake about me and the car, I would still be in school. I decided on my own to leave school because I had missed too many days which messed up my school record.

The principal should have investigated the problem thoroughly before suspending me. Then, I would not have lost out on my school work. The principal told me to study on my own and get make-up work. My case was not treated fairly.

Indeed, this is a humongous mistake for administrators to make who are entrusted five days a week with the children of the society. And the administrators must realize that suspensions are preludes to dropping out or being put out. If they realize it, they should be concerned about students dropping out. That is, they should take pride in not having African-American males to drop out of school. This would be successful administration. In the case of the respondents, following their last suspension, they remained in school one day to several months. For example, one former student got suspended the second day of the 1989-90 school term for possessing two packages of cigarettes. There were twenty cigarettes in each package and for every cigarette, they suspended him two days. Because he was suspended so long, he felt that he could not catch up with his school work. Hence, extended suspensions actually put African-American males out of high school. In another case, a respondent stated, "Once I got a five day suspension for chewing bubble gum in class. I don't understand that." He remained in school a while longer before dropping out.

They were also suspended for possession of weapons and bullets. In the case of the latter the former student said, "I found a twenty-two short bullet on my way to school. I guess somebody saw me pick it up. The administration called me to the office and suspended me ten days." Indeed, schools should not tolerate the presence of weapons and ammunition on their premises. To avoid them, the school must be excellent, in all aspects, so that students will refrain from bringing weapons and bullets to school. If a school treats its students like criminals, when they misbehave, this seems to breed in the students criminal type behavior. Hence, it is important that the legal system in the school be accurate, keen, and fair. Also, the former students were suspended for disrupting class; they talked, laughed, and joked after the teacher told them to be quiet.

School bus behavior of some African-American male dropouts also resulted in suspensions. Sometimes fights occurred at the bus stop and at other times, they allegedly violated school bus rules. For example, one respondent described his suspension related to school bus behavior. He said:

> I was on the bus and was talking to everybody. The school had already told the bus driver that I was a trouble maker. I got out my seat and talked. The driver said that I was hanging out the window, talking loud, and throwing stuff. None of it was true. I got suspended off the bus for the rest of the year. That was one more strike that made me leave school. I live too far from school to walk. To go to school, I had to get rides. They kept trying to get rid of me. I told the school officer that there was no reason to try to get rid of me because I was leaving. This was not a wise decision. They pressured me out of school. They knew that depriving me of riding the bus would cause me to stop going to school.

The interesting factor this case points out is frequent in our data. The African-American male dropout perceived his former school situation as one in which he was constantly at war with the disciplinary officer (male or female, African-American or white). According to this respondent, he and the principal did not see eye to eye. He continued:

> The principal removed my hat from my head. At first, he said that he would give it back to me, however, the disciplinary officer said for him not to give it back to me. As a result, the disciplinary officer and I engaged in a verbal confrontation. For this, I received a long term suspension. I received another suspension for "cussing" out my business teacher. Suspension serves no purpose. The student does not have the right to make up the work. It is all up to the teacher. Suspension gives students freedom to do as they please.

Again, the school setting seems to be a warfare zone. Disciplinary officers ought to be beyond reproach. And students, regardless of their tendency to be violent, should respect them. How can we expect the disciplinary officer to mete out the appropriate punishment in this case? He needs to be at least a step beyond the student. That is, he cannot afford to fight verbal violence with verbal violence. Instead, he should confront it with professionalism undergirded with caring and concern about the total situation and the results for the student.

Hanging around with the wrong people also caused them to get suspended when they were innocent. They said they were suspect by being on the scene of a fight. Also, one respondent got suspended when the computers "messed up"; only his mother could get him back in school. Later he left school. There is something about suspensions and errors on the part of the administration that took the drive out of the respondents to remain in school.

Sometimes the students pleaded not to be sent home. One of these respondents stated:

> I had a ten day suspension letter and went back to school at the end of that period. They went through my records and talked with my teachers and found two classes that I was not attending. I didn't really need the classes. After they found out about the classes they gave me ninety days because they said I did not do anything in class. They told me to come back to school May 25th. A school administrator tried to intervene but the principal would not let me stay in school. This happened even after I told the principal that I would go to all my classes. I had a lot of girlfriends at the school and they said that I was keeping them from doing their school work.

Rather than reform the student, he was put out of school. Consequently, the notion among the respondents and their mothers is that the schools suspended African-American males to get them out of the way. Without question, almost every time the administrators suspended a student they sent him on vacation. The message about suspensions, according to the respondents, is that in most cases, they should be abandoned. As one respondent put it, "Suspensions are not worthwhile. Students need mental discipline. Schools are for going to, not going from. I wanted to go to school to learn and I want to learn. Suspensions make you leave school." All African-American males should be taught to avoid suspensions because they cause them to lose their chance of graduating from high school.

School Hearings

Often suspensions were followed by a hearing at the school. Only one former student reported success in school hearings. Certainly, this raises many questions. Are the students unable to defend themselves? Do they have genuine support from the school? Are the students always wrong and the teachers always right? Are parents able to visit school and defend their children? Was every action of the former students so detrimental that they could not have received another chance? One question that emerged from the results of the hearings asked: Was justice served in the hearing? The usual answer was no. The repeated complaint was that the school officials and other members of the investigative committee would not allow them to talk. This seems to warrant enormous attention. When students are listened to, indeed they shed insight on the problem. All they say is not lies. In fact, close analysis of their comments will lead to the real problem. Similar to suspensions, it appears that a school hearing, about a problem, is the prelude to expulsion.

Expulsions

Expulsions ranged up to several months and sometimes ended the day after school closed in June. Some of the former students disagreed with the concept dropout and said they were kicked or put out of high school. According to the respondents, even when their cases were vague, they got expulsion letters. For example, one former student who got expelled the 1989-90 term said:

> I never dropped out of high school. I was put out. At my bus stop, there was a fight. A boy's girlfriend said that I had planned it. The fight was reported to the principal by one of the boy's girlfriends. While the principal was questioning all of us, the football coach was in the office. The principal gave me ten days and the others five days. I did not plan or know that the fight was going to take place. Every time I said something, the coach said that I was lying. I was suspended from January 3, 1990 to June 7, 1990.

The vagueness of this case did not seem to have any bearing on the punishment. Moreover, the principal allowed the coach to completely disrespect the manhood and humanhood of a student.

There were some dropouts who by-passed suspensions and hearings and got expelled. For example, one respondent noted, "I got expelled because a friend of mine had an illegal weapon in school and asked me to keep it. As a result, the judge gave me six months probation and a $200.00 fine. Even though I didn't have a job, I had to pay the fine within three months."

Because of the severity of punishment for wrong doing or alleged wrong doing, families need help from the school, church, and community organizations to help their children overcome actions that lead to suspensions, hearings, and expulsions. When this occurs, there will be a higher retention of African-American males in high school.

Results of Suspensions and Expulsions

The former students strongly believed that out of school suspensions should be eliminated. As far as they were concerned, they did not help. In fact, they hindered in countless ways. They made African-American males angry, stubborn, and depressed. Some of the students did not want to leave school. While they were away from school, suspensions and expulsions helped turn them into trouble makers and get a school record. According to one former student, when they get on your school record, "They take away a part of your education." Out of school suspensions sometimes caused the respondents to develop an "I don't care attitude" about school. One of these respondents stated, "Everybody tried to tell me not to be hard headed; now I see they were right. I thought that I was doing the right thing by dropping out of high school to get a job." On the other hand, the respondents agreed that out of school suspensions are warranted for such offenses as possession of fire-arms and drug dealing and using. The respondents recognized that these are patterns of behavior that cannot be tolerated by schools.

The Criminal Justice System

A few of the respondents had encounters with the criminal justice system either while they were in school, on suspension, expelled, or after they dropped out of high school. One of these cases is a runaway whose mother stated:

> My son got into trouble by being with the wrong crowd. The only problem he had was respecting authority. Most parents cannot compete with what children get in the streets by selling drugs. He made money and bought expensive things. So school was not important.

> He was in the Norfolk Detention Home and was transferred to a group home. During this time, I picked him up every day and took him to school and I haven't seen him since. He is afraid of getting caught. He owes the court time and he knows that if he comes home I'll turn him in. He has so much potential and no learning disabilities and he is very polite to most adults.

> I miss him and I'd do anything for him. I have even been to court with him and sent him to psychiatric counseling.

There were a few other respondents who had encounters with the law and often they occurred while they were suspended or expelled from school. It is likely that being put out of high school creates more rage and causes them to commit greater atrocities. Certainly, this study points up the need to eliminate suspensions, hearings, and expulsions except in the case of drugs, weapons, and ammunition.

Family Problems

Family problems were also encountered by a few of the former students. To a mother's dismay, some members of her family told her son, who is one of the respondents, "You don't have to finish school to make money." He believed them, she said, and dropped out of high school. In still another case, a son and mother did not get along. Here is how he put it:

> Mama kept arguing and putting me out of the house. I couldn't study. Mama and Daddy were having problems. She thought that I liked him better than I liked her. We didn't feel good. She never took me seriously and didn't seem interested in me. I think that she felt that way toward me because she never asked me about my school work. While I was doing homework, she started arguing. We would get in big arguments and, because I was tired and frustrated, I would miss school the next day. Mama told me to get out of her house. I stay with a friend off and on and go home when she is asleep. I do not talk with her much. The doctor said that she takes too many pills.

A mother's medication allegedly caused her to be abusive by interrupting her son's preparation for school and frustrating him so that he was neither physically nor mentally ready for school. However, there was a deeper problem. The respondent's mother appeared jealous of his relationship with his father and did not make him feel loved. Not only did she contribute to his absence but she also interfered with his sense of well being, interpersonal relationship with his father, and his education.

Parental difficulties caused another former student problems in high school. He recalls:

> When my mother and father got a divorce, I felt that I was the cause. I felt that I knew enough to make money. After four or five months went by, I realized I needed a piece of paper (diploma) saying that I had graduated from high school. I missed out and all my friends graduated. I thought that I could make it without a high school diploma, but I learned differently. I was mischievious and gave my parents a lot of problems. I made them distrust me. Not

only was I mischievous, but I lied and stole from them.

In the meantime, my parents tried to tell me that I was their darling. They have just gotten back together. I really was not the cause. The cause was something I saw going on between them. My mother had a boyfriend. After my father found out, he got a girl-friend. That hurt mama.

Mama got a boyfriend because she needed love. Mama is very af-fectionate. Daddy loves her, but he didn't show affection. She needed to hear him say, I care about you. My father is like my grandfather. That is, daddy took care of us, but didn't talk love to mama. After daddy left home, mama realized that she loved him. I am glad they are back together.

This case indicates that the respondent felt guilty for his parents' divorce and reacted to his guilt feelings by engaging in adverse behavior. The par-ents were aware of what was going on and tried to make the respondent feel cared for. The underlying problem was that the mother desired more love and attention from her husband than he provided and is perhaps a common problem in the African-American family. It is likely that more African-American males would graduate from high school if their mothers were enthralled in a loving relationship with their fathers. The freedom that such relationship would provide would give her the opportunity to focus more strongly on her children and their education. Indeed, we are suggesting that an African-American man's love for his wife is a key ele-ment in keeping the African-American male in school and obtaining a high school diploma.

And one former student had family problems with a girlfriend. The mother of his child told him that she was pregnant, but had lost it. He did not know that she was having his baby until she went into labor. Also, he thought the young woman was using birth control. She fooled him. He dated her two weeks and she became pregnant. The young woman actu-ally became pregnant after they broke up their relationship. He is very re-sponsible and does not want Social Services to take care of his child. He wants to go into the military and take out an allotment for her and the baby. Single fatherhood changed the life of a high school African-American. It appears that the African-American community should assume some of the responsibility of providing sex education for African-American males. Such education should begin at age four and last until they reach age eighteen. The idea is to grab their minds and train them to avoid single parenthood long before they become sexually active.

Indeed, these cases indicate the need for programs that help parents and children to understand and get along with each other. Also, such programs should include a component on teaching African-American males to be good sons and responsible men and women effective mothers. And the programs should convince all African-American males to respect and support each other. For example, African-American males should be reared to believe that another African-American male is too precious to be subjected to violence and mistreatment. Besides, the collective African-American male should learn to get along with non-Black males. By improving his interpersonal relations with all males, he will stay in high school and graduate. Moreover, he can achieve good interpersonal relations with other males and maintain pride as well as gain a higher status than he receives through adverse interpersonal relations.

PART IV TWELFTH GRADE MALE STAYINS

Chapter 4 African-American Male Stayins

This chapter is about successful African-American male students.It con-cerns African-American male twelfth grade stayins in the five Norfolk, Virginia high schools. This profile of African-American stayins includes their personal traits, family, school, and environment.It is concluded that each contributed to the success of the students. These stayins indicate that some students can be successful in the same settings in which the dropouts experienced difficulties that resulted in failure to graduate from high school.Therefore,the attempt is to determine personal traits and features of the settings that prevented the stayins from dropping out of school.

Personal Traits

Age

There were 238 African-American males in our total high school sample. We began with their age. It was considered important because it would in-dicate the extent of success and difficulty the respondents had experi-enced. We found that a little over 33 percent were age 17 while 46 percent were 18 years of age and 21 percent were nineteen or twenty years old (see Table 4-1). This suggests that a sizeable percentage had experienced diffi-culty passing their courses yet they were determined to get a high school diploma. Hence, unlike the dropouts, the stayins did not drop out of school because they had failed to pass their grades on time.Indeed, this is a model for all African-American males. If they find themselves falling be-hind in their grades they should use it as an incentive to work harder and stay in high school until they graduate.

TABLE 4-1: Age of African American-Male
Twelfth Grade Stayins

Age	Percent
Seventeen and younger	33.3
Eighteen	46.0
Nineteen and Twenty	20.7

Attitudes

After determining the African-American stayins' age, we sought to learn more about them by analyzing their attitude. It was conceptualized as rela-tionships (emotions and behavior) they experienced with others, including their peers. Ninety percent of them stated that a favorable attitude prevented them from dropping out of high school. Attitude is a major key to success. The development of a favorable attitude in African-American males would enable all of them to stay in school and graduate. They need a positive attitude as was manifested by the African-American male stayins in the Norfolk high schools. Also, as indicated in Table 4-2, they were more likely to be leaders (65.5 percent) than followers (30.3 percent). African-American males need to be leaders in their classes and schools. It will promote self esteem and give them status that dropouts desire but often lack. Thus, they should be encouraged by their family, church, and school to be good members and leaders of organizations. However, leadership does not necessarily mean domination; hence, only 16.8 percent stated they had a domineering attitude and only 7.6 noted they had a submissive attitude (see Table 6-2). What, in effect, can be derived from these findings is that the stayins had determination to achieve and usually made their own decisions, yet they were not domineering. When trying to get additional insight into the possible achievement they will make in life, we found that 63.4 percent stated they were ambitious while only 2.1 percent stated they were non-caring about how life turns out. Hence, unlike the dropouts, the Norfolk stayins were usually concerned about what they experienced outside school as well as in school; moreover, they desired success.

TABLE 4-2: Attitudes of African-American
Male Twelfth Grade Stayins

Attitude	Percent
Leadership	65.5
Ambition	63.4
Followship	30.3
Domineering	16.8
Submissive	7.6
Non-Caring	2.1

Educational Goals

Our profile of the African-American male stayins also focused on their educational goals. Thus, we determined their educational plans (see Table 4-3). An interesting finding is that only 6.7 percent noted they would discontinue their education with a high school diploma. As a result, the stayins were school oriented. This orientation probably contributed to their determination to remain in school as long as it took to get a high school diploma. Furthermore, it is the responsibility of the home, church,

TABLE 4-3: Educational Goals of African-American
            Male Twelfth Grade Stayins

Educational Goals	Percent
College Degree	44.9
Indefinite	11.6
Masters Degree	11.5
No Response	11.1
High School Diploma	6.7
Trade School	6.2
Doctoral Degree	4.4
Military	3.6

and school to instill the desire in all African-American males to obtain the
highest degree possible and not just an adequate education.   Education of
all African-American males will lead to a more educated race and nation.
Such achievement would reap great accomplishments for the society. For
example, an educated African-American male population would result in
fewer children born to teens and out of wedlock pregnancies thereby benefiting the entire society.

The Norfolk African-American male stayins were attempting to achieve
high educational goals. Hence, we found that the largest percent (44.9)
planned to get a college degree and ll.5 percent expected to earn a masters
degree. Unlike many African-American males, only 3.6 percent had decided to join the military. The overwhelming majority of the stayins know
what they desire to achieve educationally, however, concern is focused
on the 22.7 percent who either gave no response or said they were indefinite. These indecisive students should have received counseling and help
from teachers to develop educational goals. This finding suggests that
teachers have an enormous responsibility. Not only must they teach content the way students learn but they should teach students how to negotiate life. For example, they should especially teach students to make valuable decisions about their life. Effective decision making skills result in a
successful adult life.

Economic Goals

It follows that we asked the respondents to describe their economic
goals (see Table 4-4). Specifically, they were asked what they expected to

achieve economically? It is interesting that 43.7 percent indicated they wanted to become wealthy or comfortable rather than identify an occupation. This seems to suggest that after becoming educated, they expect to obtain occupations and own businesses that pay a great deal. The remainder of the responses to this question identified their preferred occupation. Of this group, the largest percentage desired white collar occupations (14.8 percent) and professional occupations (14.0). For the most part, these stayins had set sound economic goals. Yet, there were 15.2 percent of the respondents who either did not respond to the question or did not know what they wanted to become in life. Indeed these students also needed counseling that would have enabled them to determine what they wanted to achieve economically in life. All African-American males should establish achievable economic goals that will make them self-sufficient. Besides, they should have the work ethics firmly established in their thinking to enable them to make their economic goals a reality.

TABLE 4-4: Economic Goals of African-American Male Twelfth Grade Stayins

Economic Goals	Percent
A Comfortable Life	29.7
A White Collar Occupation	14.8
Wealth	14.0
A Professional Occupation	14.0
Military	7.2
A Blue Collar Occupation	5.1
Indefinite	2.5
No Response	12.7

The Meaning of Success

It was also important to determine what success means to the stayins. We asked them a series of questions to get their response and told them to check as many answers as applied. Their answers were solidly mainstream (see Table 4-5). Thus, the most important indicator of success was getting a good paying job (98.3percent). The implication of this finding is that the African-American male stayins were work oriented. Therefore, they counteract the stereotype of the shiftless African-American male. Instead, they are men who rate a good paying job a top priority. The other chief indicators of success to the respondents and in this order were earning a high school diploma (96.6 percent), getting a good job (95.1 percent), buying a home (93.3 percent), and excellent work on some job (92.3 percent). Also, earning a college degree (84.5 percent), owning a car (84.3 percent), having friends like themselves (74.9 percent), and getting married and then having children (68.8 percent) were indicators of success.

It can therefore be concluded that the African-American males who had reached their senior year in high school had adult goals, including a college education, and made adult decisions. When the collective African-

TABLE 4-5: The Meaning of Success to African-American Male Twelfth Grade Stayins

Types	Percent
A Good Paying	98.3
High School Diploma	96.6
A Good Job	95.1
House Purchase	93.3
Excellent Work	92.3
College Degree	84.5
Car Purchase	84.3
Compatible Friends	74.9
A Family	68.8

American male establishes and pursues these priorities, dropping out of school will no longer exist.

The Family

Residence of Stayins

To provide greater insight into the profile of African-American male twelfth grade stayins, inquiry was made about their family life. In discussing the family of the African-American male stayins, emphasis was placed on the person they lived with (see Table 4-6). Did they live with both parents or one parent? We found that 6.5 percent lived only with their father while 50 percent lived only with their mother as parent. Yet, out of the 238 respondents, 90 lived with both parents. Certainly the family structure had some cracks in it, but close to half of the respondents lived

with both parents. In the stayins' population, we see a strong family structure coupled with a broken structure. Hence, we do not have the usual
portrait of the African-American family. Moreover, only one respondent
lived with someone other than a father, a mother, or both parents. We,
therefore, concluded that the families of stayins were relatively strong.

TABLE 4-6: Residence of African-American
Male Twelfth Grade Stayins

Live With	Percent
Mother	50.0
Both Parents	39.5
Father	6.5
Other	4.0

The Most Important Person in Their Life

To obtain a better understanding of family life, the respondents were also
asked to identify the most important person in their life (see Table 4-7).
There was a wide range of persons who had important relationships with
the respondents.   Sixteen percent chose their father while 64 percent
chose their mother as the most important person in their life. Another kinsman who was the most important person in the life of a few seniors was
their grandmother (6.9 percent). Then some stayins (10.4 percent) chose
someone other than their parents, grandparents, or siblings as the most im-

TABLE 4-7: The Most Important Person in the
Life of African-American Male
Twelfth Grade Stayins

Person	Percent
Mother	64.1
Father	16.0
Grandmother	6.9
Grandfather	1.7
Older Sibling	0.4
Other	10.4
Unidentified	0.4

portant person in their life. When the total picture is put into perspective, a few stayins chose their fathers as the most important person in their life and a female kinswoman was the most important person in the life of 71 percent of the respondents. This means that the African-American high school senior males in the Norfolk setting had a more meaningful relationship with a cross-sex than same-sex parent or grandparent. Yet, they did not let it prevent them from reaching the senior class. This finding suggests that some single parents have the skills to help their children remain in high school until the twelfth grade.

Siblings

Still another element in the profile of the African-American stayins' family concerns their siblings (see Table 4-8). A higher percent (33.2) did not have sisters than did not have brothers (25.2). Among the respondents with siblings, the largest percent of the respondents had only one brother (35.9) and or one sister (31.9). Moreover, a relatively large percent (19.7) had three or more brothers and 15.5 percent had three or more sisters.

TABLE 4-8: Siblings of African-American Male Twelfth Grade Stayins

Number	Sisters	Brothers
None	33.2	25.2
One	31.9	35.9
Two	19.4	19.2
Three of more	15.5	19.7

Birth Order Position

Still another element in the profile of the African-American male stayins' family concerns their birth order. As shown in Table 4-9, the birth order

TABLE 4-9: Birth Order of African-American Male Twelfth Grade Stayins

Birth Order	Percent
First	35.9
Second	25.6
Third	14.1
Other	24.4

varied among the African-American stayins.The largest percent (35.9) were first born children and the second largest percent (25.6) were second born; however, a sizeable percent of the stayins were fourth born or higher.

Siblings' School Dropout History

Because the respondents had stayed in school, we desired to know whether their siblings had also stayed in school. As shown in Table 4-10, we determined whether a sibling of either sex had dropped out of school and, if so, how many? It was determined that 24.3 percent of the respondents had at least one brother to drop out of school while only 12.6 percent of the respondents had a sister who had dropped out of school. The findings indicate that the respondents had experienced a larger percent of their brothers than sisters dropping out of school. Thus it appears that Af-

TABLE 4-10: Educational Status of African-American Male Stayins' Siblings

Status	Brothers	Sisters
Dropped Out	24.3	12.6
Did Not Drop Out	75.7	87.4

rican-American males are at higher risk of dropping out of school than African-American females.

Greater understanding of the family was determined by the grades the respondents' siblings dropped out of school (see Table 4-11). Starting in the sixth grade, the stayins' brothers began to drop out of school. In middle school (seventh and eighth grades), there was a noticeable increase in the percent of the stayins' brothers who dropped out of school.In the ninth through twelfth grade (high school) their brothers had dropped out of school in alarming proportions; and the tenth grade was their most vulnerable year.

On the other hand, the African-American male stayins' sisters began dropping out of school in the middle grades and continued throughout high school (see Table 4-ll).Though a high percent of their sisters dropped out in high school, the most vulnerable year was the eleventh grade.When the vulnerable tenth grade year of the respondents' male siblings is compared with the vulnerable eleventh grade year of their female siblings, their female siblings dropped out more frequently. These findings indicate that in the family of some stayins there is also a school dropout problem. Therefore, families and teachers should take continuous precautionary measures to prevent males and females from dropping out of school. And dropout preventions should begin as early as elementary school.

TABLE 4-11: Grades Siblings of African-American
Male Stayins Dropped Out of School

Grade	Brothers	Sisters
Sixth	2.8	0.0
Seventh	0.0	2.3
Eighth	4.3	0.0
Ninth	21.4	16.3
Tenth	27.1	16.3
Eleventh	22.9	30.2
Twelfth	18.6	18.6
College	0.0	2.3
No Response	0.0	13.9

Parental Schooling

Because these students were stayins, we were interested in finding out how much schooling their parents had, whether their parents worked, and the type of work they did. We began with their schooling (see Table 4-12). The highest percent (32.2) of the respondents' fathers were high school graduates or had some college education (30.4 percent); and only 5.6 percent had less than some high school education. Similarly the highest percent of the respondents' mothers were either high school graduates (36.8) or had some college training. One factor that is immediately visible is that even though the mothers of the respondents had more schooling, the gap

TABLE 4-12: Education of African-American
Male Stayins' Parents

Education	Father	Mother
Less Than High School	5.6	3.5
Some High School	11.7	9.2
High School Graduate	32.2	36.8
Some College	30.4	29.4
College Graduate	20.1	21.1

is almost closed between fathers and mothers who had received some college training.

Another important point is that the parents of the stayins were relatively
well educated. In fact 21.1 percent of their mothers and 20.1 percent of their
fathers were college graduates. This seems to make another point about
their parents; that is, not only did they have a similar college education but
they also chose mates who were like themselves. This latter factor and the
good education of the parents were probably strong enough to help the
respondents become high school stayins.

Parental Employment

As noted earlier, the inquiry also focused on whether the respondents
were from families where parents worked (see Table 4-13). It was found
that 84.1 percent of their fathers and 79.2 percent of their mothers worked.
Essentially, the stayins were from homes where fathers and mothers
worked. Seeing their parents work probably had an effective impact on
the future work orientation of the stayins and contributed to them staying
in school. Strong families of this type, with a working father, are likely to
muster enough strength not only to keep their sons in school, but to see
that they graduate and go to college.

TABLE 4-13: Work Status of African-American
Male Stayins' Parents

Employment Status	Father	Mother
Employed	84.1	79.2
Unemployed	15.9	20.8

Parental Occupations

Their parents worked in a variety of occupations (see Table 4-14). They
ranged from professional occupations to retirement.The largest percent of
the fathers were employed in blue collar occupations while the highest
percent of the mothers were employed in white collar occupations. And a
sizeable percent ofthe mothers were employed in professional occupations.

The Family's Role in Preventing Stayins from Becoming Dropouts

Next, we turned to the role of the family in preventing the African-
American male twelfth grade stayins from dropping out of school. We
found that parents, siblings, and relatives were concerned about the respondents. Parents, especially, had so much control over some of the respondents until they said their parents would not let them drop out of
school.There were also those parents who told the respondents that a high

TABLE 4-14: Occupations of African American
Males Stayins' Parents

Occupations	Father	Mother
Professional	7.0	16.9
White Collar	14.0	24.2
Blue Collar	35.0	17.8
Service	0.0	5.1
Military	6.2	0.0
Housewife	0.0	0.4
Retired	0.8	0.0
Unidentified Occupation	14.0	11.9
Unemployed	10.7	9.7
No Response	12.3	14.0

school diploma was important to achieving a good job or a college education. Moreover, their parents wanted them to graduate from high school
because they were having a "rough time" and they desired their children to
have a better life than they had experienced. And there was the refrain,
"Make something out of yourself," from their mothers that kept them from
dropping out of school. These parents made a point of having their sons
understand that to become successful, they needed an education. And
they made success an attractive word in their conversations.

In other cases, the father and mother sat down and discussed the importance of education and encouraged the respondents to get their high
school diploma. For example, one respondent noted, "I know that one reason I stayed in school is that my parents explained to me the importance of
staying in school. They always told me that life would not be easy and
that I was preparing for any hardship that I might face. Whenever I had a
problem in school, they always had time to help me."

There were other parents who only had to encourage or influence the
respondents to remain in school, be caring, and provide all types of support. Moreover, some parents inspired their sons to want a happy life--
meaning money--and that money results from an education. And, of course,
a number of mothers "pushed" their sons to get them to the senior class.
How? They made certain they awakened early enough to go to school

and went to school everyday or almost everyday.

Then, parents, especially mothers, threatened their sons. For example, one respondent's mother said, "If your grades drop, I will make you quit sports" and another mother promised to kill her son if he quit school while a few mothers threatened to put their sons out of the house if they dropped out of high school. One respondent put it this way, "If I dropped out of school, my parents and other family members would probably make it hell for me." Some respondents stayed in high school because they wanted to be the first in their family to get a high school diploma and a college education; they wanted to complete what they had started.

There were other family reasons that explain why several respondents did not drop out of high school. They include the following:

> One of the reasons that I stayed in school was because my brothers and sisters set good examples and I followed their example.

> The reason I did not drop out of high school was because I felt that I owed a high school diploma to my parents and myself.

> My father really stressed education to my brother, sister, and myself. It would be disrespectful and shameful not to get a high school diploma. And I don't want a nickel and dime job. I want to live large.

> I have not dropped out of school because of my father. Before he died, he told me how proud he would be when my diploma is hanging on the wall beside his. Now he'll never see my diploma, but I know when I get it, it will be something like granting his final wish.

> I stayed in high school because I wanted to do the opposite of what my father wanted me to do.

> I have a good grandmother and father.

> I don't want to let my parents down. Also, none of my brothers is successful and I want to be successful.

> I guess the most important thing that caused me not to drop out of high school was my family. They helped me with my teachers and were patient. I wasn't forced to be the best in the class, but my parents just asked me to do my best.

> I didn't drop out because I knew that it would hurt my mother and

disappoint my father.

I didn't drop out of high school because my family seems to know what is best for me. I follow their lead.

My mom and my family tree have kept me in school.

My family has no quitters.

I stayed in school because my mom said I couldn't make it. I am proving that I can.

The embarrassment of not being able to complete something as simple as high school is just beyond my self-esteem. I would laugh in the face of one who couldn't do that simple task. They should be able to do it even if they are in a class of 500.

One implication of these findings is that if parents can prevent older children from dropping out of school, it becomes a model for younger children. Therefore, it is important that young mothers know this so they will not make a mistake in rearing their first child. Once the pattern of success is set in motion, the remainder of the children in the family are likely to imitate it. The responses of the stayins also indicate they respected their parents and their family. We can also abstract from the respondents' relationship with their family a great deal of love and caring. There was mutual love between parents and children. Indeed, both are important to the success of African-American high school males. Hence the respondents' family was most important in keeping them in high school.

Personal Determination

The second most important reason that kept the stayins in school was their own desire to obtain a high school diploma. In all probability this determination was instilled in them by their family. As one respondent stated, "I want to be all that I can be. To be rich. To be known worldwide for what I do in the music world, to be a star." Also, obtaining a high school diploma was a way to find their identity. For example, one respondent noted, "What basically kept me in school was patience, determination, and curiosity to see what I will become and what I will do in life. I am curious to see how I will accomplish it." These stayins also said they had goals in life, things they wanted to achieve, and the desire to be the first in their family to get either a high school diploma or a high school diploma and a college degree.   They also said, I want to become a military officer and a good provider for my family to fulfill the craving I have to become successful in life and make my mother and myself proud. To conclude, one respondent noted that he did not want to be a laborer all his life. He continued,

"Being a Black male today is hard and I believe that we can overcome the drugs and easy money that lure us away from school, if teachers encourage students to do better, call their parents when the students are not doing their lessons, and become more involved with the students who are poten- tial dropouts. Most students who drop out feel they are dumb and are scared to show they don't know as much as the next person." Indeed, this respondent reinforces the need for clearer and more extensive and sound teaching in the classroom to circumvent the dropout problem. Furthermore, he suggests the importance of teacher involvement with students beyond the classroom. He sees teachers as a bridge between the family and school that will help African-American males stay in school and graduate.

The High School

Because we had studied African-American male dropouts, we wanted to understand the stayins' school experiences (see Table 4-15). Did the school help them become twelfth grade students? To answer this question, we in- quired about what the school had done to prevent the respondents from dropping out. For example, we asked whether understanding what teach- ers were teaching kept them in school and 52.5 percent answered in the affirmative. Then, approximately the same percentage, 52.9, noted that un- derstanding the teachers' assignments helped keep them in school and 39.1 percent explained that extra school assistance helped. A related finding is that 42.4 percent of the respondents were kept in school in part because they were assigned subjects that held their attention. Further, 65.5 percent stated that making good or passing grades helped keep them in high school. Indeed, it is clear that making good grades is an incentive for stay- ing in school. This sends a clear message to students and educators alike; they should work together and see that African-American males make good grades. After students work, they desire the grades they deserve. Only about half (45.8 percent) of the stayins indicated they received the grades they deserved; but the remaining 54.2, who believed their grades were unfair, did not let that cause them to drop out of school. Nevertheless, administrators should set the tone in their school that insists on each student, including African-American males, getting the grades they deserve. By telling African-American males this is white and Black racism, they will know to fight the situation and not just accept what the teachers say. When unfair grading occurs, teachers should be required to prove it, not alone by the grades in the roll book, but by reevaluation of papers-- work performed.

According to 47.5 percent of the African-American male stayins, as- signment to excellent teachers helped keep them in school. It seems clear that one way to hold African-American males' attention and keep them in- terested in their school work is to assign them the best teachers in school. These teachers will hold their interest, educate them, and help them graduate.

TABLE 4-15: Behaviors That Kept African-American Male
Stayins From Dropping Out of School

Techniques	Percent
Parental Emphasis on Learning	68.9
Made Passing or Good Grades	65.5
Teachers Liked Them and Cared	65.1
Friends Were Not Adverse to School	53.8
Understanding Assignments	52.9
Understanding Teaching	52.5
Teachers Complimented &Patted Them on the Back	48.7
Excellent Teachers	47.5
Received Grades Deserved	45.8
Assigned Subjects That Held Attention	42.4
Received Extra Study Help	39.1
Compatible Friends	30.7
Other Reasons	30.3
Teachers Did Not Blame Them for Disturbance	19.7
Assigned Male Teachers (Disciplinarians)	17.6

We turned our attention more specifically to teachers to ascertain clearly their role in helping these African-Americans to be stayins. Over half (57.6 percent) noted that having teachers who gave them attention helped keep them in school. And an even larger percent (65.1) of the 238 African-American male stayins said that having teachers who liked them and were caring helped keep them in school. These stayins are saying very vividly that African-American males need excellent teachers and teachers who pay them some attention and are warm and caring. This is further reinforced by 48.7 percent of the respondents who noted that having teachers who complimented them on their work and patted them on the back helped keep them in school. It does not appear that race of student, type of class, and type of school are the answer to keeping African-American students in school. Instead, they will stay in school, with a first class teacher of any color.

These stayins were not usually blamed for disturbance in class. Only 19.7 percent noted that not being blamed for disturbance helped keep them in school. Nevertheless, this is an important finding; African-American males do not like to be blamed for classroom disturbance. If they are found wrong, an effort should be made, on the part of the teacher, to correct it. Less emphasis should be placed on blaming the student and more emphasis on correcting the problem.

The African-American male stayins also noted other positive ways the schools kept them from dropping out. A few stated the following:

> The reason that I did not drop out of high school is because I had very nice teachers that helped me with my work when I needed help. I had the nicest friends that I got along with.

> I had the best track coach and I could trust him.

> I had the best financial aid counselor who helped me get money for college.

> I received an art scholarship.

> Certain teachers taught me to fight and never give up.

> I had teachers who pushed me to do everything I could to pass my courses.

> I have so many teachers who helped me out.

> Being at school is where I fit in just right.

> I stayed in school because I have been involved in a lot of activities such as the summer Governor's School, Cooperating Hampton Roads Organization for Minority Engineers (CHROME) and the Strolling Silver Strings. With these activities, I am very busy. Also, going to church has taught me the wrongs and rights of life.Next, I want to become an engineer. We need more minorities in this field.

> National Junior ROTC gave me the will to strive to be the best possible person I could be. By being understanding, my teachers helped in many ways. I think that my parents have influenced me in a way that it would be crazy for me not to succeed in life. I

would also like to see NJROTC around in the coming years, but Congress has not entered it in their budget. And I think that it will hurt a lot of high school children whom NJROTC could help academically.

One of my teachers who was very caring told me not to drop out of high school.

I always liked school. My teachers always depended on me for certain things.

These stayins indicate that feeling needed by teachers, caring teachers, and activities helped keep them in school. Even the slightest comment from a teacher can make a difference between dropping out of school and earning a high school diploma. The Junior ROTC has also made remarkable contributions to the stayins. It especially helped them to become disciplined and strive for success. Because Junior ROTC is valuable to all students perhaps the Congress of the United States will decide to reinstate the program.

Some of the athletic respondents stayed in school to play sports. For example, one respondent stated, " I think the main thing that kept me from dropping out of school was sports. I like sports a lot and playing high school sports has kept me off the streets and these days the streets are a bad place to be." They worked hard to maintain the required two point grade average to remain on the teams. The coaches also had a great deal of influence over their lives. One respondent said, "I owe my education to all my coaches." Another respondent described his life thusly:

When I was little, I looked forward to going to Booker T. Washington High School and playing basketball. And I got that chance. Everyone looks up to me.

The Norfolk Public High Schools gave some of the stayins a good experience. In return, the respondents accepted it and stayed in high school. Also, the schools helped some of them obtain scholarships to continue their education. There are two important factors involved: the school, especially the teachers and counselors, helped the respondents to succeed; and those who did not receive help had the stamina and family support to remain in school. Hence, these successful stayins had a very different high school experience than the dropouts. The stayins' experience should be the model for all African-American male high school students.

Environment

Along with their personal traits, family, and school, the African-American stayins' environment helped keep them in school. For example, a respondent talked about the larger society. He stated: "I know this white system we live in wants us, the Black man, to drop out of school so they can give reasons for not paying us as much as they pay their own people. There are many reasons I didn't drop out of high school, but that is the main one." This respondent used racism to his advantage. Rather than only complain about racism, it is a good thing to use it as an incentive to be the best that one can become.

However, the remainder of the respondents who commented on the environment talked about their own neighborhoods or the ones they had seen. For example, two selected responses about environment as a motivating factor to stay in school follow:

> I saw there was no reason to drop out. I saw a lot of people who had dropped out of school. They're either selling drugs, working at a corner store, or in jail. Most of them are selling drugs. They're my friends, but they did not influence me. I don't even let my peers pressure me to smoke and drink. One time I needed some money and didn't have a penny. My friend asked me if I wanted to sell drugs to make some. I refused.

> I don't want to be like the people on the streets. Students are dropping out of school because they get in trouble in school and teachers and personnel don't care about their future or try to help them, so they just take the easy way and put them out. The ones that are put out find there's nothing to do in the house so they go in the streets and get paid in full for drugs. When its time to come back to school, they have expensive cars and jewelry. Teachers and personnel get jealous and give them a hard time, which causes them to stay home and make more money. It's not always the case that they don't want an education, it is just that they don't feel like being hassled.

This respondent is suggesting that teachers and administrators contribute to the drug problem. In other words, if the school personnel were kinder to returnees following suspensions, that may keep them in school. It appears that the school needs to hold drug treatment seminars for administrators and teachers to teach them how to lessen the participation of African-American males in the drug culture. Moreover, teachers could benefit from seminars that teach them how to relate to student drug dealers which could result in the cessation of drug dealing and more interest in school.

There were other stayins who noted that their environment helped keep them in school. They stated:

I have seen a lot of people with no education who are nothing but drunks. It is very upsetting because most of them are of the Black race. This is why the other part of the society (whites) degrades us. So this has pushed me to another level to advance my studies as a college graduate.

I live in a very wide open project area where I see guys and gals ages 17-50 on drugs, walking the streets, and standing on store corners and this is something I wish not to do. Therefore, I'm going to stay in school and accomplish something out of life.

The thing that caused me not to drop out of school was the environment around me.My brothers stayed in trouble, but they wanted me to be different. They will not let me fight, drink, or even do drugs. I am in school today and love each and every one of my brothers for that. I feel sorry that it is hard for them to change, but they are trying very hard.

I just looked at some other people and saw how bad they were looking and doing and it pushed me more. If I have no interest in my life, how can someone else care?

When I walked the streets and saw people bumming and sleeping on the streets and wearing the same clothes everyday and depending on churches for food, it made me stay in school.

The most important factor in my decision not to drop out of high school is that I looked around and saw people who didn't finish school and realized that I had to finish to keep from being like them.

When I go to the store, I see bums and alcoholics begging for money. I see people turn into drug addicts. I didn't want to turn out like that.

The African-American high school male seniors used their environment to advance themselves. Rather than conform to its ways, they rebelled. In reality, the environment made them more interested in getting a high school diploma. These findings indicate that youthful African-American males rose above their environment and stayed in high school. This is a marked contrast to the African-American male dropouts. To put the whole picture in perspective, it is clear that some students are swallowed up by devastating environments while others rise above them and become a success. What makes the difference? The personal traits of the students and a strong family and school support system maintain students in school.

Other Reasons That Kept the Respondents in School

Personal traits, family, school and environments contributed to keeping the African-American males in high school. Besides, there were various other reasons that explain why some African-American students did not drop out of high school. They stated:

> I saw everybody else who had graduated; I wouldn't feel right if I didn't do the same.

> Church taught me the rights and wrongs of life.

> My attitude. I know what I want in the future.

> What I start, I always finish.

> Friends and girlfriends pushed and encouraged me.

> Knowing the Lord. He has put a positive attitude in my life.

> I wanted to become someone and not a bum on the streets.

> A drastic improvement in my grades.

> I have two friends I hang around with that joke and if I drop out of high school they will joke me about not having anything in life.

> Faith in God in everything I do.

> To keep alive the dream of my forefathers and what they went through to get us Black people to this point.

> Good friends who are interested in what I say and do.

Also, 53.8 percent noted that having friends who did not influence them to drop out of school helped keep them in school. In general, findings about friends suggest that these achievers were kept in school in part because there was no peer pressure to drop out. Indeed, this finding encourages parents to attempt to get their children to associate with others like themselves.

The high school stayins were not only perceptive, but they used their knowledge for their personal betterment.

Chapter 5 White Male Stayins

This Chapter is the counterpart to Chapter 4. It profiles the personal traits, family, school, and environment of white male twelfth grade stayins in the five Norfolk, Virginia High Schools to determine what maintained them in high school.

Personal Traits

Age

There were l66 white male seniors present in the five high schools the day we administered the questionnaire and, therefore, they comprise our sample. They were a somewhat young group of seniors. Hence 45.7 percent were age seventeen while 43.3 percent were age eighteen and only ll.0 percent were age nineteen or twenty (see Table 5-l). Hence, in general, they were successful from the standpoint of their age and grade.

TABLE 5-1: Age of White Male Twelfth Grade Stayins

Age	Percent
Seventeen and younger	45.7
Eighteen	43.3
Nineteen and Twenty	11.0

Attitudes

Desiring to know more about the respondents, we asked them about their attitude. We were especially interested in finding out whether their attitude (emotions and behavior) helped prevent them from dropping out of school. We found that 83 percent of the l66 respondents considered their attitude important for keeping them in school.   There were varied traits that comprised their personality (see Table 5-2), including leadership. More than half, 53 percent, of the respondents stated they had a leadership attitude. When they were asked whether they had a followship attitude, only 2l.7 percent answered affirmatively. Because only a small percent stated they were followers, the insight these findings suggest is that even the respondents who did not have a leadership attitude tended to control their life. Yet, the followers needed guidance to make certain they continued to follow the people who believed in their family values and the values of society. Were the respondents ambitious was another question asked. And we found that 63.9 percent stated they were ambitious while only 6.0 percent noted they had a non-caring attitude about what occurs

TABLE 5-2: Attitudes of White Male Twelfth
Grade Stayins

Attitude	Percent
Ambition	63.9
Leadership	53.0
Followship	21.7
Domineering	21.7
Non-Caring	6.0
Submissive	6.0

in their life. Yet, the non-caring respondents should not be in that category; if they are not ambitious, they should be caring. This is where the counselor and teacher can make a difference by their teaching style and counseling techniques. In general the respondents had neither a domineering nor followship relationship. Indeed, both characteristics can contribute to success.

TABLE 5-3: Educational Goals of White Male
Twelfth Grade Stayins

Educational Goals	Percent
College Degree	44.8
Masters Degree	13.9
Doctoral Degree	10.3
High School Diploma	9.7
Indefinite	9.1
Trade School	4.8
Military	0.6
No Response	6.7

Educational Goals

Because the respondents were in their senior year, we desired to find out whether they had further educational goals (see Table 5-3). They were asked about their college plans. We found that 44.8 percent indicated they planned to go to college; and 58.7 percent indicated they would get either a college, masters, or doctoral degree. Indeed, well, over a majority of them planned to continue the educational success they had realized almost twelve years.

Economic Goals

The economic goals of the white male stayins were also determined (see Table 5-4). Rather than identify an occupation, 21 percent indicated their economic goal was wealth and 28.8 percent noted they desired a comfortable life style. Among those who identified their preferred occupation, the largest percent (15.3) desired a professional occupation. Only 2.8 percent were indefinite about what they desired economically; hence, almost all the white male stayins had definite economic goals.

TABLE 5-4: Economic Goals of White Male
Twelfth Grade Stayins

Economic Goals	Percent
A Comfortable Life Style	28.8
Wealth	20.9
A Professional Occupation	15.3
A White Collar Occupation	14.7
A Blue Collar Occupation	7.3
Military	3.4
No Response	6.8
Indefinite	2.8

The Meaning of Success

After ascertaining the economic goals of the the students, we asked them a series of questions related to success (see Table 5-5). We desired to know what they considered success. One interesting finding is they planned to be a working population. Hence, 94.5 percent noted that success means getting a good paying job. They made a distinction between a good paying job and a good job; therefore 92.5 percent said that getting a good job was related to success. In line with getting a good job and good wages, they intend to do excellent work (93.1 percent). An even higher percentage (95.6) indicated that earning a high school diploma represented success. It is therefore no small wonder that they remained in high

TABLE 5-5: The Meaning Of Success to White
Male Twelfth Grade Stayins

Types	Percent
High School Diploma	95.6
A Good Paying Job	94.5
Excellent Work	93.1
A Good Job	92.5
College Degree	87.3
House Purchase	86.5
Compatible Friends	83.4
Car Purchase	81.2
A Family	72.0

school for they cherished a high school diploma. Buying a home was not as important to them as having a good paying job; thus 86.5 percent indicated that success, to them, was related to buying a home. Also, earning a college degree was not as important to them as a good paying job and a high school diploma, for only 87.3 percent noted that it is related to success. Similarly owning a car (81.2 percent) and having friends like themselves (83.4 percent) were not as important as a good job, a good paying job, and a high school diploma. Relative to the preceding factors, marriage and a family were not as highly related to success; only 72 percent indicated they considered it important to success. Thus, most respondents focused on those factors that will help them get ahead economically and occupationally. Moreover, perhaps the respondents took a good marriage and family for granted. In other words, perhaps they were considered rewards of success.

The Family

Residence

Beside personal traits, family behavior helped keep the respondents in school. Did the respondents live with both parents, one parent, or a significant other?(see Table 5-6). We found that 67.1 percent lived with both parents while 22.6 lived with their mother and 6.3 percent lived with their father. Hence, a large percent of the white male stayins lived with both parents which probably contributed to their success in high school.

TABLE 5-6: Residence of White Male
Twelfth Grade Stayins

Lives With	Percent
Both Parents	67.1
Mother	22.6
Father	6.3
Other	4.0

The Most Important Person in Their Life

Since a majority of the respondents were in two parent families, we determined whether they were closer to their mother or father (see Table 5-7). The most important person in the life of the largest percent (35.8) was their father. It is also interesting that eight of the respondents considered a sibling to be the most important person in their life. Moreover, 25.8 percent of the respondents noted that the most important person in their life was someone other than their parents, siblings, and grandparents. This suggests that a large number of respondents may not have a particularly close relationship with their parents--at least not as close as with some other significant person; but they have a close relationship with at least one positive other.

TABLE 5-7: The Most Important Person in White
Male Twelfth Grade Stayins' Life

Person	Percent
Father	35.8
Mother	30.2
Older Sibling	5.0
Grandmother	1.9
Grandfather	1.3
Other	25.8

Siblings

To provide a better understanding of the respondents, we asked about their siblings (see Table 5-8). We found that the largest percentage (37.4) did not have any brothers while the smallest percentage (9.2) had three or more brothers; however, 35.6 percent had one brother. In general, a considerably large percent did not have any brothers and those respondents with a male sibling usually had only one or two brothers. A smaller percentage (36.7 percent) did not have any sisters; similarly a larger percentage (45.2) had one sister.

TABLE 5-8: Siblings of White Male Twelfth Grade Stayins

Number	Sisters	Brothers
None	36.7	37.4
One	45.2	35.6
Two	10.8	17.8
Three of more	7.2	9.2

Birth Order Position

Another line of inquiry concerned birth order position. Were these older or younger children in their family? As indicated in Table 5-9, a large percentage (44.2) of the white male stayins was first born (44.2 percent) or second born (26.1 percent) children (see Table 7-2). Essentially they were the older children in the family. Nevertheless, 29.7 percent of the respondents were third born or higher.

TABLE 5-9: Birth Order of White Male Twelfth Grade Stayins

Birth Order	Percent
First	44.2
Second	26.1
Third	17.6
Other	12.1

Siblings' Dropout History

We also desired to know whether any of their siblings had dropped out of school (see Table 5-10). We found that 11.2 percent of their brothers and 12.4 percent of their sisters had dropped out of school. Nevertheless, none of the siblings of the stayins dropped out in elementary and middle school.

The grades in which the siblings dropped out of school were also determined (see Table 5-11). The most vulnerable year for their brothers was the tenth grade. Hence, 44.4 percent of their brothers who dropped out of

TABLE 5-10: Educational Status of White Male
             Stayins' Siblings

Status	Brothers	Sisters
Dropped Out	11.2	12.4
Did Not Drop Out	88.8	87.6

school did so in that grade. On the other hand, the most vulnerable years
for their sisters who dropped out were the eleventh and twelfth grades.
Their sisters suggest the need to monitor females even after they get promoted to the twelfth grade. It is also shown that the second most vulnerable year for the brothers to drop out was the twelfth grade in which 27.8
percent dropped out. Similarly, the third most vulnerable year of dropping
out for the sisters was the tenth grade in which 22.2 percent dropped out.

TABLE 5-11: Grades Siblings of White Stayins
             Dropped Out of School

Grade	Brothers	Sisters
Sixth	0.0	0.0
Seventh	0.0	0.0
Eighth	0.0	0.0
Ninth	16.7	11.1
Tenth	44.4	22.2
Eleventh	11.1	27.8
Twelfth	27.8	27.8
College	0.0	11.1
No Response	0.0	0.0

Parental Schooling

     The profile of the white stayins' family also includes their parents'
schooling (see Table 5-12). The largest percent of the respondents' fathers
were either college graduates (31.8 percent) or high school graduates (31.1
percent). Only four respondents (2.6 percent) had fathers with less than
some high school education. The same pattern was true of their mothers.
Hence, the largest percent of their mothers were college graduates
(34.6 percent) or high school graduates (32.7 percent). In general the respondents had parents who were almost evenly matched in education.

Besides, their parents were an educated group. Relatively well-educated parents contributed to family strengths and probably encouraged the respondents to succeed in high school.

TABLE 5-12: Education of White Male Stayins' Parents

Education	Father	Mother
Less Than High School	2.6	1.9
Some High School	12.6	9.6
High School Graduate	31.1	32.7
Some College	21.9	21.2
College Graduate	31.8	34.6

Parental Employment

Work was next in the profile of the respondents' families. We desired to know whether their parents worked (see Table 5-13). We found that 7.4 percent of their fathers did not work while 92.6 percent worked. Because their mothers were ranked almost evenly with their fathers in education, we desired to know whether they worked. We found that more mothers than fathers did not work. Yet, a sizeable percentage (71.8) worked and 28.2 percent did not work. Thus, the respondents generally came from two career homes.

TABLE 5-13: Work Status of White Male Stayins' Parents

Employment Status	Father	Mother
Employed	92.6	71.8
Unemployed	7.4	28.2

Parental Occupations

The parents of the respondents were employed in varied occupations. For example, as shown in Table 5-14, the fathers of the respondents were employed in professional, white collar, blue collar, and military occupations. However, the largest percent (32.9) were employed in white collar occupations and some of them had retired. Similarly, with the exception of the military, the working mothers were employed in the same occupations along with service work (3.0 percent). The largest percent (30.5) of the respondents' mothers were employed in white collar occupations. An unusual finding is that 20.7 percent of the respondents did not respond to this question.

TABLE 5-14: Occupations of White Male Stayins'
Parents

Occupations	Father	Mother
Professional	12.2	17.7
White Collar	32.9	30.5
Blue Collar	16.5	9.8
Service	0.0	3.0
Military	11.0	0.0
Housewife	0.0	1.8
Retired	1.8	0.0
Unidentified Occupation	15.2	8.5
Unemployed	5.5	7.9
No Response	4.9	20.7

The Family's Role in Preventing Stayins from
Becoming Dropouts

To complete the family profile, we determined the role that it had played
in keeping the respondents in school. The motivation of their parents
was significant to preventing the Norfolk, Virginia white male twelfth
grade stayins from dropping out of school. They said such things as if I
had dropped out of high school, "My parents would have killed me" and
"My parents would kick my butt!!!" Two other respondents stated, "My
parents told me that if I wanted the better things in life I had to finish
school and go to college" and "My parents want me to succeed to a better
life and support them in the long run." Another respondent noted, "The
main thing that made me stay in school was my father and sports. My father always expected a lot from me in the classroom, on the football field,
and wrestling mat." Yet, still another respondent stated, "Although my
mother dropped out of school, my father went to college and became highly successful, and since I lived with him, while growing up, it must have
rubbed off. I have also been in gifted schools and programs since elementary school age, and I think those schools really allow you to expand and
stay interested." And another respondent noted, "I didn't want to let my
mother down. I wanted to prove to those who thought I would drop out

wrong for my self-esteem." Another stayin noted, "If I dropped out of school, my brother would kick my a..." Yet, still another respondent stated, "When it came to school work, my parents were very strict on me. They also helped me a lot with problems in school, but I also had will power." Another said, "If I were to drop out of school, my family would drown me and then have me executed." Also, one respondent's father told him he had to stay in school because he was not stupid enough to dropout. The parents were actively involved in keeping the respondents in school. It appears that this is a major solution to keeping students in school. Parental involvement should begin as early as kindergarten and continue until college graduation.

Personal Determination

Even though the family of the respondents was influential in keeping them in school, it was determined that personal desire was an important reason that prevented them from dropping out of school. When they talked about personal desire, they noted that an education was essential to their goals. They desired good paying jobs, success and education; and had an inner motivation to excel. For example, one respondent stated, "I have pursued a good education to get a good paying job and a decent life after graduation. Also, I realize that dropping out of school would guarantee a poor, miserable life without many luxuries." Moreover, a few of them had made promises to themselves that they would not drop out of high school. Further, some respondents related they had a passion for knowledge; they wanted to know everything.

Indeed, the respondents had personal determination to stay in school along with strong encouragement from their parents. Thus, the family and students were important to high school male achievement and retention.

The School

We also desired to know the role of the high school in keeping the respondents in school (see Table 5-15). Therefore, they were asked whether understanding their teachers' kept them in school. Forty-four percent stated that it contributed to their staying in school. A larger percentage (47.6) of the respondents noted that understanding assignments was more important than understanding the teacher. Similarly, receiving extra help with studying (38.6 percent) was important to keeping the respondents in school. More important than any of these factors was making passing or good grades. Hence, 68.1 percent indicated they had stayed in school for one or both of these reasons. This leads us to conclude that success in school is closely tied to staying in school. On the other hand, there did not seem to be as much concern about getting the grades they deserved. Only 43.4 percent noted that it was related to staying in school. An even smaller

TABLE 5-15: Behaviors That Kept the White Male Stayins
From Dropping Out of School

Techniques	Percent
Parental Emphasis on Learning	69.9
Made Passing or Good Grades	68.1
Teachers Liked Them and Cared	61.4
Teachers Gave Them Attention	52.4
Friends Were Not Adverse to School	59.6
Understanding Assignments	47.6
Understanding Teaching	44.0
Teachers Complimented/Patted Them on the Back	44.0
Excellent Teachers	48.8
Received Grades Deserved	43.4
Assigned Subjects That Held Attention	44.6
Received Extra Study Help	38.6
Compatible Friends	39.2
Teachers Did Not Blame Them for Disturbance	16.9
Assigned Male Teachers (Disciplinarians)	16.9
Other Reasons	46.4

percentage (39.2) linked staying in school with having friends who made
good grades. But it was important to 59.6 percent to have friends who did
not influence them to drop out of school. Being assigned subjects that
held their attention was only important to 44.6 percent in terms of influ-
encing them to stay in school. The respondents were almost evenly divided on the factor that excellent teachers were important to staying in
school. Similarly, we did not find a large percentage (16.9) who said that
having male teachers who could maintain order was related to keeping
them in school.

When asked about the personal characteristics of teachers as related to keeping them in school, we found an interesting result. That is, 61.4 percent indicated that teachers who liked them and were caring helped keep them in school. Another interesting finding is that 52.4 percent indicated that teachers who gave them attention helped maintain them in school while 44.0 percent noted that teachers who complimented them and patted them on the back helped keep them in school. Although they are young men, the respondents suggest the importance of warm and loving teachers to student retention. Apparently, they were not blamed much for classroom disturbance because only 16.9 percent indicated that being taught by teachers who did not blame them for classroom disorder was related to staying in school.

Other Reasons That Kept the Respondents in School

There were varied other reasons that explain why the white male seniors in Norfolk, Virginia stayed in school. They stated:

> My girlfriend and my sister helped keep me in school. My sister graduated from the University of Virginia and is going to Harvard and doing well. I want to be just like her. New cars, money, trips, etc. And, also if you don't have an education, it is very hard to get a good job.

> My desire to learn.

> I don't consider myself stupid, ignorant, or just plain dumb. Those are the types that drop out.

> Parents, friends, sports, good attitude, and knowing that an education is now important in society.

> I understand that it is a privilege to be taught.

> I meet lots of females and go out with them. There is nothing better to do during the school year. Also, I play sports and like beating up other teams.

> I am involved with the soccer team which I am very good at. Another reason I stayed in school is that I am in the Norfolk Public Schools Arts Repertory in which I am an actor. This is why I have managed not to drop out of school. Also I have stayed in school because of help from my friends.I can make better friends in school and have better knowledge of everything and prepare for my future life.

> The people I hang around with at this school are more academical-

ly centered rather than party/drug centered. I never had any feelings about dropping out. My background from a private school
kept me in high school without any thoughts of dropping out.

My friends, my family, and the attitude of not giving up and just
sticking in until the end of high school; and I think the willingness
to succeed prevented me from dropping out of school.

I didn't want to drop out because I'd seen others who had and
where they are today. Friends see mistakes and I try not to be like
them.

An inner motivation to excel in school. This is necessary because
many teachers are unable to maintain the students' interest in the
classroom.

My parents were a great influence and the military structure of
NJROTC caused me to stay in school. NJROTC hasn't been
planned for the 1991 FY-Budget. This valuable course should be
kept in the national school curriculum as a deterrent for potential
dropouts.

My father's success.

Good friends or people who were interested in what I had to say
or do.

More importantly, thinking socioeconomic status as a white, middle class person, influenced me greatly. I feel that a solution to the
problem of dropping out is the proposal of the proposition: prison
or school?

I knew I didn't want to work at a fast food restaurant or get into
drugs so I just kept going to school.

My determination not to be beaten and be called a quitter caused
me to stay in school.

All my family members have graduated or are graduating from college. Getting a good education was always a priority instilled in
us (my sisters and myself) since childhood. After my mother died,
graduating from high school and college have an extra meaning to
me.

The thought of being a loser and never getting a job caused me to
stay in school.

I stayed in school because I want to make something successful of myself.

I didn't drop out of school because I want to be smart and own a Jaguar, a house, and money.

I stayed in school because I like to see my friends on a daily basis. I like the free lunches, too.

I just don't see where dropping out of school would get me.

I had excellent teachers who gave me attention and knew their lessons in my subjects. They also complimented me for a job well-done.

I think I stayed in school mainly because of the academic environment. I have participated in accelerated classes all my life and have been "bred" to compete. I want happiness for myself and I know the only way to achieve this happiness is to get an education which will prepare me for a successful career.

When I was born my mother was very young (16). Because of this, many in her family said that I would be a failure in life. I stayed in school to show them that a 16 year old with enough sense of responsibility can raise a successful young man.

I stayed in school because I don't want to be a statistic.

These responses indicate that the respondents had pride and desired to achieve success. Their personal determination, interest in knowledge, desire for the good life, strong parents, effective teachers, and school-oriented friends kept them in high school. Therefore the combination of strong personal traits, strong families, effective teachers, and helping friends prevented the white male stayins from dropping out of school. These are traits, if applied, that should keep all males in high school.

PART V DETERMINING A POTENTIAL HIGH SCHOOL MALE DROPOUT

Chapter 6 How to Determine a Potential African-American Male Dropout

This chapter compares the findings on African-American male drop-outs, African-American male stayins, and white male stayins to determine a profile of a potential high school dropout. These findings are also used to compare African-American and white male stayins.

Personal Traits

Age

Starting with age, as shown in Table 6-1 the dropouts were younger than the stayins. To understand this finding the grade levels of the dropouts must be described. They ranged from the ninth to the twelfth grade while all the stayins were in the twelfth grade. Moreover, the data in Table 6-1 indicate that the African-American male stayins were older than the white male stayins. Thus, the African-American male dropouts were the youngest on average and the African-American stayins the oldest. One vivid point is that while only 11 percent of the white male stayins were nineteen or twenty years old 20.7 percent of the African-American male stayins were the same age. There is not much difference between the African-American male stayins and white male stayins in age category eighteen, but, again, there were vivid differences, between them, in the seventeen and younger group of males in the twelfth grade. Not only were there differences between the stayins, but as suggested by the data in Table 6-1, a potential dropout is one who is at least one grade behind in his school work.

TABLE 6-1: Age

Age	African-American Male Dropouts %	African-American Male Stayins %	White Male Stayins %
17 and under	54.3	33.3	45.7
18	31.4	46.0	43.3
19 - 20	14.3	20.7	11.0

Attitudes

The attitudes of the respondents were also compared (see Table 6-2).

Regarding attitude toward leadership, African-American male stayins considered themselves leaders more often than white male stayins. Beneath their surface, there is an African-American male who wants to be recognized; he wants to be somebody significant. Another vivid point about leadership is that the dropouts characterized themselves less often than both races of stayins as being leaders. African-American stayins are 50 percent more likely than African-American dropouts to see themselves as leaders. When an African-American male does not appear to be interested in leadership that is reason enough to keep track of him to determine whether he is becoming a dropout.

Followship is another area of comparison. The most glaring finding is that the African-American male respondents are more likely to be followers although less than half of all respondents claim to be followers. This suggests that a strong peer--friend could influence some African-American males not to attend school and to engage in deviant behavior. Thus, the African-American males who were followers represented potential dropouts. Moreover, the dropouts were less ambitious than African-American male stayins and white male stayins. Also, they were much more non-caring about the outcome of life. Yet, they were more often both domineering and submissive than the stayins. When these three traits were found in the respondents they indicated that they were possibly at risk for becoming dropouts. Overall, the dropouts ranked highest on non-positive characteristics and lowest on the positive characteristics. On the other hand, when we compared the two groups of stayins, they were very similar; they were more similar to each other than African-American male dropouts and African-American male stayins. This suggests that the negative attitudinal traits identified here were indicative of potential dropout behavior.

TABLE 6-2: Attitudes

Type	African-American Male Dropouts %	African-American Male Stayins %	White Male Stayins %
Leadership	44.3	65.5	53.0
Followship	41.5	30.0	21.7
Ambitious	56.6	63.4	63.9
Non-Caring	24.5	2.1	6.0
Domineering	34.9	16.8	21.7
Submissive	34.9	7.6	6.0

Because attitude is important, the stayins were asked whether their attitude kept them in school. It was found that 90 percent of the African-American male stayins agreed that it had helped them stay in school and 83 percent of the white male stayins noted that it had kept them in school. The question was asked in the reverse to the dropouts. Of the dropouts, 35.8 percent stated their attitude had caused them to drop out of high school. It seems important to teach good attitudinal behavior in the home, school, church, and community for an unfavorable attitude signals a potential dropout.

Educational Goals

The African-American male stayins and the white male stayins had similar educational goals (see Table 6-3). The highest percent of both groups of stayins,more than 50 percent, desired a college degree or a masters degree. The African-American male stayins and white male stayins had higher educational aspirations than the African-American dropouts (see Table 6-3).

TABLE 6-3: Educational Goals

Educational Goals	African-American Male Dropouts %	African-American Male Stayins %	White Male Stayins %
High Sch Diploma	28.8	6.7	9.7
Trade School	5.0	6.2	4.8
GED	22.5	0.0	0.0
Associate Degree	1.2	0.0	0.0
College Degree	28.8	44.9	44.8
Masters Degree	0.0	11.5	13.9
Doctorate Degree	0.0	4.4	10.3
Medical Doctor	1.2	0.0	0.0
Military	0.0	3.6	0.6
End of Education	7.5	0.0	0.0
Indefinite	5.0	11.6	9.1
No Response	0.0	11.1	6.7

More than half of the dropouts desired a high school diploma or G. E. D. Moreover, 7.5 percent stated they would not pursue additional education and 5.0 percent did not know their educational plans. Even so, all the dropouts cannot be put into two or three categories. Hence, some of them desired to achieve a high level of education. In this group, 28.8 percent desired a college degree. Low educational aspirations are perhaps a sign that African-American males are a potential dropout. Nevertheless, many of them desire a good deal more education.

Furthermore, a higher percent of the white male stayins than African-American male stayins planned to end their education with a high school diploma. One explanation for this finding is that white male high school graduates can obtain more lucrative jobs than African-American male high school graduates. On the other hand, a higher percentage of African-American male stayins than white male stayins had decided to pursue a trade career. However, approximately the same percentage planned to get a college education. Moreover, approximately half of both samples desired a college degree. Hence, the stayins of both races were college oriented; further, more than 10 percent of each sample desired to attend graduate school.

Economic Goals

In regard to economic goals, again, the African-American male stay-ins and the white male stayins were similar (see Table 6-4). Economically, the highest percent in each category desired a comfortable life style. And both

TABLE 6-4: Economic Goals

Economic Goals	African-American Male Dropouts %	African-American Male Stayins %	White Male Stayins %
Wealth	0.0	14.0	20.9
Comfortable	0.0	29.7	28.8
Professional	2.5	14.0	15.3
White Collar	38.0	14.8	14.7
Blue Collar	25.3	5.1	7.3
Military	19.1	7.2	3.4
Indefinite	24.1	2.5	2.8
No Response	0.0	12.7	6.8

groups had a sizeable percent of males who desired to be wealthy. None of the dropouts expressed an interest in wealth or comfort. Moreover, a relatively small percent of the stayins planned to work in blue collar occupations compared to one-fourth of the dropouts. While the dropouts were least likely to show interest in the military, among the stayins, more than twice as many African-American males as white males chose the military. Nevertheless, the economic goals of the African-American stayins were high. They were notably higher than the economic goals of the African-American male dropouts. When economic goals are high that can be a sign that students will be stayins through high school graduation.

The Meaning of Success

Also, we determined the success model for each study population and the populations are amazingly similar (See Table 6-5). In ranked order, the African-American male dropouts considered the following to be the five most important achievements to represent success: a good job, a good paying job, a high school diploma, excellent work, and purchase of a home. The African-American male stayins chose essentially the same five factors with a slightly different ranking: a good paying job, a high school diploma, a good job, excellent work and a college degree. Similarly, the white male stayins chose the following achievements to represent success: a high school diploma, a good paying job, excellent work, a good job, and a college degree. And for all three groups, compatible friends and a family are

TABLE 6-5: The Meaning of Success

Success	African-American Male Dropouts %	African-American Male Stayins %	White Male Stayins %
Good Job	86.3	95.1	92.5
Good Paying Job	84.5	98.3	94.5
High School Diploma	80.7	96.6	95.6
Excellent Work	80.2	92.3	93.1
House Purchase	76.8	93.3	86.5
College Degree	63.3	84.5	87.3
Car Purchase	55.8	84.3	81.2
Compatible Friends	60.5	74.9	83.4
A Family	47.5	68.8	72.0

important to success.

The Family

Residence

As indicated in Table 6-6, we also determined the residence of the respondents. We found that more of the white male stayins were from two parent families while a larger percent of African-American male stayins and African-American male dropouts came from homes with only the mother present. Moreover, a larger percent of the African-American male dropouts lived with someone other than their parents than the stayins in both races. The conclusion here is that children from single parent homes and who live with someone other than their parents are more likely to drop out of school than children from two parent families; however, there are numerous exceptions.

TABLE 6-6: Residence

Lived With	African-American Male Dropouts %	African-American Male Stayins %	White Male Stayins %
Father	6.6	6.5	6.3
Mother	58.5	50.0	22.6
Both Parents	23.6	39.5	67.1
Other Person	11.3	4.0	4.0

The Most Important Person in the Respondents' Life

Another area of comparison focuses on the most important person in the respondents' life. As noted in Table 6-7, the mother of African-American male dropouts and stayins was the most important person in their life. Approximately two-thirds of each group gave this response. The father was the most important person in the life of the white male stayins. The percent of white male stayins who said their father was the most important person in their life is more than twice as high as the African-American male stayins and almost ten times higher than the African-American male dropouts. A higher percent of white male stayins had a close relationship with a male figure than the African-Americans. Besides, the mother is only slightly more important in the lives of the white stayins than a significant other. That brings us to the next point; the white male stayins had significant others more often than African-American male stayins. Yet, there is something important about the African-American stayins.They were strongly linked to a maternal figure, mother or grand-

TABLE 6-7: The Most Important Person in
                    Respondents' Life

Person	African-American Male Dropouts %	African-American Male Stayins %	White Male Stayins %
Mother	67.0	64.1	30.2
Other Person	17.9	10.4	25.8
Father	3.8	16.0	35.8
Older Sibling	3.8	0.4	5.0
Grandmother	2.8	6.9	1.9
Grandfather	0.9	1.7	1.3
Not Identified	3.8	0.4	0.0

mother, and less highly linked with a significant other. This indicates the strength of the mother-son relationship in the African-American family. Comparing the three groups, the dropouts had a closer relationship with their mother than African-American and white male stayins. It seems safe to conclude that when males are linked closely to their mothers rather than to their fathers, it is important to monitor their school work; they can either be successful or dropouts. The surest way to keep African-American males in school is for them to come from a two parent home.

Family Size

Family size was another area of comparison among the African-American and white males (see table 6-8). The African-American male stayins and

TABLE 6-8: Number of Respondents' Male Siblings

Number of Siblings	African-American Male Dropouts %	African-American Male Stayins %	White Male Stayins %
None	23.6	25.2	37.4
One	27.4	35.9	35.6
Two	22.6	19.2	17.8
Three or More	26.3	19.7	9.2

dropouts had more brothers than the white male stayins. One vivid example is that there were more white stayins who did not have brothers than African-American stayins. However, in regard to dropouts and stayins with one or two brothers, the African-American male stayins were more like the white male stayins than the African-American male dropouts. These findings suggest that children with a large number of brothers are potential dropouts and should receive continuous help and attention from their family, school, and church.

Family size as shown in Table 6-9 also included inquiry about the number of sisters of the respondents. An interesting pattern is shown. High school male dropouts were more likely to have sisters or to have more sisters than African-American male stayins and white male stayins. Again, overall, the African-American stayins were more like the white male stayins than the African-American male dropouts. Nevertheless, the point that we do not want to overlook is that when an African-American male has any number of sisters, he is more likely to be a potential dropout. Perhaps when there are daughters, the African-American family places more emphasis on their education than the education of sons. If this is the case, the pattern needs to be corrected; African-American families should place equal emphasis on educating their sons and daughters. And education should be second only to religion in child-rearing.

TABLE 6-9: Number of Respondents' Female Siblings

Number of Siblings	African-American Male Dropouts %	African-American Male Stayins %	White Male Stayins %
None	18.9	33.2	36.7
One	32.1	31.9	45.2
Two	28.3	19.4	10.8
Three or More	20.7	15.5	7.2

Birth Order

The inquiry also focused on birth order position. As can be seen in Table 6-10, there was some variation in order of birth. For example, the white male seniors were more frequently first born than African-American males. Further, white male seniors were in the second or third birth order position more often than African-American males. Though the white male stayins varied from the African-American male stayins, the birth order of African-American male stayins and dropouts is very similar. Yet, there is one important difference; African-American male stayins had a higher percentage of first born than the dropouts. Perhaps first born males, compared to others, stay in high school and graduate.

TABLE 6-10: Birth Order of Respondents

Birth Order	African-American Male Dropouts %	African-American Male Stayins %	White Male Stayins %
First	30.5	35.9	44.2
Second	22.8	25.6	26.1
Third	16.2	14.1	17.6
Other	28.6	24.4	12.1
No Response	1.9	0.0	0.0

Sibling Dropout History

To get clearer insight into the respondents' family life, we determined whether their brothers had dropped out of school (see Table 6-11). A smaller percentage of the white male stayins had brothers who had dropped out of school than the African-American male stayins and dropouts. And unlike the African-American males, there was no white male respondent who had three or more brothers to drop out of school. Moreover, when African-American males had brothers who had dropped out of school, that seemed to put them at risk of dropping out. Further, the African-American male stayins and white male stayins were more similar in terms of not having brothers to drop out than African-American dropouts.

TABLE 6-11:Percent Who Had Male Siblings To Drop Out of School

School Status	African-American Male Dropouts %	African-American Male Stayins %	White Male Stayins %
Dropped Out	34.9	24.3	11.2
Did Not Drop Out	60.4	75.7	88.8
No Response	4.7	0.0	0.0

To round out the picture of dropping out of school in the respondents' families, we asked whether their sisters had dropped out of school (see Table 6-12). One finding concerning sisters of respondents who had dropped out of school was that African-American male stayins and white male stayins were more similar than the African-American male stayins and dropouts. Nevertheless, when the African-American male respondents had more than 15 percent of their sisters to drop out of school, they were a potential dropout.Thus, it appears that when a sizeable percentage of sisters of African-American males has dropped out of school, counselors should

TABLE 6-12: Percent Who Had Female Siblings To Drop Out of School

School Status	African-American Male Dropouts %	African-American Male Stayins %	White Male Stayins %
Dropped Out	18.9	12.6	12.4
Did Not Drop Out	75.5	87.4	87.6
No Response	5.6	0.0	0.0

implement behaviors to hold African-American males in school. Sisters who are dropouts signal the possibility that their brother is a potential dropout and the counseling department should circumvent it.

Next, we compared the percentage of brothers of the respondents who had dropped out of school. According to Table 6-13, the African-American male stayins were more similar to the white male stayins in hav- ing only one brother to drop out of school than to the African-American male dropouts. On the other hand, the African-American male stayins were more similar to the African-American male dropouts in terms of two or more of their brothers having dropped out of school. This table suggests that African-American males are vulnerable to dropping out of school and special school programs and effective teaching should be designed and implemented to keep them in school.

TABLE 6-13: Number of Male Siblings Who Dropped Out of School

Number	African-American Male Dropouts %	African-American Male Stayins %	White Male Stayins %
One	48.9	64.2	65.0
Two	24.4	24.5	35.0
Three or More	2.2	11.3	0.0
No Response	24.4	0.0	0.0

Similarly, we compared the percentage of sisters of the respondents who had dropped out of school (see Table 6-14). The largest percent of the African-American male dropouts and stayins and white male stayins had one sister who had dropped out of school. When determining what per- cent of the respondents had two or more sisters who dropped out of school, it was found that the African-American male stayins surpassed the African-American male dropouts and white male stayins. Indeed, this find-

TABLE 6-14: Number of Female Siblings Who Dropped out of School

Number	African-American Male Dropouts %	African-American Male Stayins %	White Male Stayins %
One	53.8	48.0	68.4
Two	7.7	36.0	26.3
Three or More	3.8	16.0	5.3
No Response	34.6	0.0	0.0

ing suggests that African-American males can be successful in homes where sisters are school dropouts. Also, it suggests the vulnerability of the respondents' sisters to dropping out of school. It is thus concluded that African-American public school children of both sexes should be the re-cipients of effective teaching and counseling that keep them in school.

Grades Respondents' Brothers Dropped Out In

Of the respondents who had brothers to drop out of school, particular grades were most vulnerable (see Table 6-l5).   While 8 percent of the Afri-

TABLE 6-15: Grades Male Siblings Dropped out of School

Number	African-American Male Dropouts %	African-American Male Stayins %	White Male Stayins %
5	2.1	0.0	0.0
6	0.0	2.8	0.0
7	0.0	0.0	0.0
8	6.4	4.3	0.0
9	21.3	21.4	16.7
10	21.3	27.1	44.4
11	21.3	22.9	11.1
12	14.9	18.6	27.8
College	0.0	1.4	0.0

can-American dropouts and 7 percent of the African-American stayins had brothers who dropped out of school before the ninth grade, none of the white stayins had brothers leaving school so early. The ninth through the eleventh grades were the three most vulnerable years for the brothers of African-American male dropouts and stayins while the most vulnerable grades for the brothers of the white male stayins were ninth, tenth and twelfth; the tenth grade was extremely vulnerable for the brothers of the white male stayins. Still another finding is that the twelfth grade was a vulnerable school term for the brothers of African-American male stayins and dropouts and white male stayins. This suggests that African-American males and white males continue to need quality counseling in the twelfth grade. Furthermore, when African-American males have brothers who dropped out in high school, special academic attention should be given to those males to prevent them from becoming a dropout.

Grades Respondents' Sisters Dropped Out In

Similarly, of the respondents who had sisters to drop out of school, all high school grades were vulnerable years (see Table 6-16). A larger percent of the sisters of African-American male dropouts had dropped out in the eleventh grade and the tenth grade than in the remaining two grades; the largest percent dropped out in the eleventh grade. According to the African-American male stayins, the largest percent of their sisters dropped

TABLE 6-16: Grades Female Siblings Dropped out of School

Number	African-American Male Dropouts %	African-American Male Stayins %	White Male Stayins %
5	0.0	0.0	0.0
6	0.0	0.0	0.0
7	0.0	2.3	0.0
8	0.0	0.0	0.0
9	12.5	16.3	11.1
10	20.8	16.3	22.2
11	25.0	30.2	27.8
12	12.5	18.6	27.8
College	0.0	2.3	11.1

out of school in the eleventh grade. For the white male stayins, the most vulnerable grades for their sisters were the eleventh and twelfth. These findings suggest that females of both races need to be targeted with programs that maintain them in high school.   Moreover, when African-American male students have a high percent of sisters who have dropped out of school this is an indication they may drop out of high school.

Parental Education

Education of parents is also related to students dropping out of school. The educational level of fathers of African-American male dropouts, African-American male stayins, and white male stayins was almost equal from entering high school through high school graduation, but the education beyond this point was very unequal (see Table 6-17). A larger percent of the parents of the stayins had more college training than the parents of the dropouts. Hence, African-American males who drop out are more likely to have fathers who have a high school diploma. Also, the fathers of the dropouts were more likely to have less than a high school education. On the other hand, African-American male stayins and white male stayins are more likely to have college educated fathers.

TABLE 6-17: Education of Respondents' Fathers

Education Of Fathers	African-American Male Dropouts %	African-American Male Stayins %	White Male Stayins %
Less Than High School	10.5	5.6	2.6
Some High School	14.3	11.7	12.6
High Sch Graduate	39.0	32.2	31.1
Some College	5.7	30.4	21.9
College Graduate	3.8	20.1	31.8
Unknown	26.7	0.0	0.0

When we analyzed the mother's education, we found that a larger percent of mothers of African-American male stayins and white male stayins had more education than the mothers of the African-American male dropouts (see Table 6-18). More of the dropouts had mothers with less than a high school education and some high school education than the mothers of the stayins. Yet there was little difference between stayins and dropouts in terms of mothers who had received a high school diploma.

TABLE 6-18: Education of Respondents' Mothers

Education Of Mothers	African-American Male Dropouts %	African-American Male Stayins %	White Male Stayins %
Less Than High School	9.5	3.5	1.9
Some High School	27.6	9.2	9.6
High Sch Graduate	35.2	36.8	32.7
Some College	17.1	29.4	21.2
College Graduate	2.9	21.1	34.6
Unknown	7.6	0.0	0.0

Nevertheless, African-American male dropouts had a smaller percent of mothers with some college training or a college degree than the stayins of both races. The data for the dropouts are somewhat limited because all the males did not know the educational level of their parents. However, it seems clear that low paternal and maternal educational levels are associated with dropping out of high school.

Another noteworthy comparison relates to the family in general. That is, the parents in each study population were almost equally matched in educational attainment. Therefore, we must make certain that these parents with low educational attainment do not pass on to their children the same pattern; instead, they should educate their children.

Work Status of Parents

Still another family comparison is the work status of the respondents' parents. A higher percent of the fathers of white male stayins were working than of African-American male stayins and dropouts (see Table 6-19). It

TABLE 6-19: Work Status Of Respondents' Fathers

Employment Status	African-American Male Dropouts %	African-American Male Stayins %	White Male Stayins %
Employed	64.2	84.1	92.6
Unemployed	13.2	15.9	7.4
Unknown	22.6	0.0	0.0

follows that the fathers of the African-Americans were the more unemploy-ed group. It appears that a higher percentage of the fathers of the African-American stayins was unemployed than of the African-American dropouts. Of course, one of the drawbacks in this table is that the dropout respons-dents did not always know the work status of their parents. One other thing seems certain; the African-American male dropouts had the lowest proportion of employed fathers.

As also shown in Table 6-20, when the mothers' work status was deter-mined, a similar pattern emerged. The mothers of the high school dropouts had the lowest percent of employment while the mothers of the African-American stayins had a higher employment rate than the mothers of the white male stayins. It appears that unemployment of mothers was closely related to the dropouts leaving school.

When the parents of the stayins were compared, it was determined that their father and mother were not equal breadwinners. A larger percent of the fathers in both stayin groups worked than the mothers of the stayin groups. And the fathers of the white male stayins were employed consid-

TABLE 6-20: Work Status Of Respondents' Mothers

Employment Work Status	African-American Male Dropouts %	African-American Male Stayins %	White Male Stayins %
Employed	63.2	79.2	71.8
Unemployed	31.1	20.8	28.2
Unknown	5.7	0.0	0.0

erably more often than the mothers of the white male stayins. Though there was a difference between the parents of African-American male stayins' parents, the employment gap was not very large.

Behaviors That Kept the Stayins in School

After determining how personal traits and family are linked to potential dropouts, we asked the stayins what factors had kept them from dropping out of school. As can be seen in Table 6-21, there was close agreement between the African-American male stayins and white male stayins. There were various reasons that kept the respondents in school. For purposes of this comparison, we chose the five principal reasons that kept the stayins in school. In descending order, the African-American male stayins agreed that parental emphasis on learning, passing or good grades, teachers who liked them and cared, teachers who gave them attention, and friends who were not adverse to school helped prevent them from dropping out. Similarly, in descending order,the white male stayins indicated that parental emphasis on learning, making passing or good grades,teachers who liked them and cared, friends who were not adverse to school, and teachers who gave them attention were the most important factors that kept them in school. Close scrutiny of the factors that kept the stayins of both races in school indicates that parental emphasis on education and success and caring teachers were important to maintaining students of both races in school.

TABLE 6-21: Behaviors That Kept The Male Stayins in School

Behaviors	African-American Male Stayins %	White Male Stayins %
Parental Emphasis on Learning	68.9	69.9
Made Passing or Good Grades	65.5	68.1
Teachers Liked Them and Cared	65.1	61.4
Teachers Gave Them Attention	57.6	52.4
Friends Were Not Adverse to School	53.8	59.6
Understanding Assignments	52.9	47.6
Understanding Teaching	52.5	44.0
Teachers Patted Them On The Back	48.7	44.0
Excellent Teachers	47.5	48.8
Received Grades Deserved	45.8	43.4
Assigned Subjects That Held Attention	42.4	44.6
Provided Extra Study Help	39.1	38.6
Compatible Friends	30.7	39.2
Not Blamed For Disturbance By Teachers	19.7	16.9
Assigned Male Teachers (Disciplinarians)	17.6	16.9
Other Reasons	30.3	46.4

Behaviors That Would Have Prevented the Dropouts from Leaving School

We also asked the same questions to the African-American male dropouts in reverse (see Table 6-22). We asked what techniques would have prevented them from dropping out of school. In descending order, they stated that the five most important factors were better grades and subjects that held their attention, excellent teachers, extra help with school work, compliments on their work, and more attention from their teachers would have prevented them from dropping out of school. Hence, the dropouts desired the same treatment from their teachers as the stayins re-

TABLE 6-22:   Behaviors That Would Have Prevented African-American Male Dropouts From Leaving School

Behaviors	%
Better Grades	51.7
Subjects That Held Attention	51.7
Excellent Teachers	48.3
Extra Help With Home Work	41.4
Different Group of Friends	36.8
Teachers Who Complimented Their Work	34.5
More Attention From Teachers	32.2
Understanding the Teaching	28.7
Teachers Who Liked Them	25.3
Friends Who Made Good Grades	25.3
Getting Deserved Grades	24.1
Teachers not Blaming Them For Classroom Disturbance	24.1
Male Disciplinarians As Teachers	19.4
More Parental Emphasis On Education	14.9
No Preventive Technique	1.1

ceived.   Besides, a great deal more was needed to keep the African-American males from dropping out of high school. For example, under-standing what the teachers were teaching was important to retention. This can be accomplished through clear statements, examples, and a caring attitude. Moreover, to get students to learn, they must feel liked--a feeling that teachers should convey to all students. Therefore, teachers should maintain a classroom that does not have an adversarial tone. And male teachers are not a prerequisite for a congenial classroom.   In fact, only 14.9 percent of the dropouts indicated the need for male disciplinarians as teachers. However, more parental emphasis on education is needed. This requires that teachers serve as a bridge between the school and home. Because poor school performance is closely associated with dropping out of school while high performance is clearly identified with staying in school, it appears that teachers would utilize their knowlede and personal achievements to help African-American males, as well as other students, realize their full potential in high school and graduate on time.

Conclusion

This chapter has provided ways to determine a potential dropout and emphasized the importance of working with such students to prevent them from leaving school. Moreover, it has shown factors that maintained African-American males and white males in high school until the second semester of their senior year. Further, it has compared the study popula-tions and it is concluded that the stayins of both races are more similar than the African-American male stayins and African-American male dropouts.

Chapter 7 Multi-Level Social Policy

This study has presented a description of African-American male dropouts and a comparison of African-American male dropouts, African-American male stayins, and white male stayins to determine how to retain African-American males in the public school system. The analyses and comparisons of these three study populations contribute to our understanding of high school African-American males' behavior and the obstacles they face. Also, the three studies indicate ways to retain African-American males in high school and ways the stayins were prevented from dropping out of high school. The results of these analyses suggest policy solutions on the federal, state, school, community, church, family, and personal levels.

Starting with the federal government, there needs to be a federal commission on African-American male public school students. It should hold semi-annual meetings to assess the status of African-American male high school students and recommend national legislation. The policy should include college scholarships to deserving graduating African-American male seniors as an incentive to keep them in school. Also, the policy should include a gun control law that punishes males, ages 14-24, who have guns in their possession. This recommendation should be implemented immediately because African-American teenage high school students are shooting and killing each other. Moreover, the commission should organize state commissions and require semi-annual reports on in-school African-American male problems and successes and utilize them as the basis for recommending additional federal and state legislation.

Based on findings in this study, there is also a great deal that state governments can do to maintain African-American males in high school. For example, they should integrate all levels of their public schools. Simultaneous with integration, states should establish initiatives that result in schools that educate all students for further intellectual pursuits and to negotiate life. Black schools are not the answer. In Black schools, teachers and students are isolated from the American mainstream. Yet they must negotiate it. Furthermore, when some students leave Black schools they are insecure in competition with white students. The exceptions are not the issue here. The concern is with the collective African-American male. Not only a few African-American males, but all African-American males should realize their full potential. When the whole person is educated, in effective integrated schools, this is likely to become a truism. Black schools educate only a part of African-American males while effective integrated schools educate them for life. It is incumbent upon the state to educate African-American males and all students for life and give them a world class education.

To develop effective schools, state governments should make changes in their high school curriculum. For example, there should be a required social science course in anti-violence for all students. Such course should reduce school violence by 30 to 40 percent. A related course that should be required of all students is race relations. Although the Civil Rights Revolution of the 1960s gained some rights for African-Americans, racism is not dead. It is expanding in the lives of non-white minorities, especially African-Americans. The most dreadful thing about racism is that African-American males experience it while they are developing into manhood. While teenagers, they experience racism in the workplace, criminal justice system, and school room. Indeed, racism is tough enough on African-American adults, but it is even tougher on teenage African-American males.

The concern here is with racism in the school. African-American males are still called "boy" by some white teachers and get sent to the office for the slightest deviation from rules. White adult school administrators retort that African-American males must learn to deal with being called "boy" or say it is just a figure of speech. It is more than a figure of speech to African-American teenagers; it strikes sparks off them. They are men and want to be recognized as young men. Similarly, the African-American disciplinarian takes the accused African-American male student in his office and makes an excuse for suspending or expelling the student by saying, "You knew better." This is a cop out without any disciplining creativity to help the student. One policy issue here is to assist administrators in dealing effectively with African-American male students. Another policy issue is to help young white Americans and African-Americans develop mutual tolerance. A related policy issue is development and integration of effective schools on all public school levels.

Another curriculum need is a module, in all United States and State history courses, on the contributions of African-Americans to American and state history. This module should include inventors and their inventions, scientists and their discoveries, African-American social movements and their leaders, historical and contemporary leaders, and the changes they helped bring about in the American society.

Still another curriculum need that could be implemented by the state is to provide an elective course in entrepreneurship. Rather than sell drugs, African-American males should be taught how to make something to sell. It could be wood, metal, glass, leather, or upholstered products.

Further, another policy recommendation for state governments is that they require students to attend school year round with a two week vacation. A related policy suggestion is that the required age for attending school be extended to eighteen. Refusal to obey the law should be punishable by labor without compensation. Another policy recommendation is that the state make available gold cards for all students who make the honor roll two consecutive semesters. These gold cards should serve as an incentive to study.

Other state policy suggestions concern administrators and colleges. College education departments should be required to teach a course in public school disciplining. In turn, the state should require all current and future disciplinary officers, principals, and teachers to take a three hour credit course in disciplining African-American students and other minorities. Should the school disciplinarian officer be trained for his job? Or, should he be promoted from teacher to assistant principal? Should a teacher be trained in classroom disciplining as well as course content? These questions are relevant to policy. Moreover, colleges and universities should sponsor summer institutes that train principals, assistant principals, and teachers to be good disciplinarians. That is how to bring out the best and not the worst in African-American male high school students.

There are also policies that should be implemented by high schools. They include a sound anti-drug program. Drugs are an alarming problem among African-American high school males. They are sold in men's restrooms and outside gymnasiums or cafeterias. There is a comprehensive policy that can be put into effect that will break up drug dealing and using in schools. For example, each school should have cameras in male restrooms and monitors in male principals' offices. Also, young dropouts, who are former drug users should be recruited by the school system to serve as undercover agents. To break up the school drug syndrome, arrest one or two drug dealers and users as examples. Besides, school systems should hire police to guard our children on the school grounds. Moreover, it should be the policy of all schools to present anti-drug programs several times a year. These school assemblies should include reformed drug dealers and users. They should describe the cruelty of drugs and punishment for offenders which should act as deterrents to students. African-American males often engage in adverse behavior, such as drugs, because they do not truly understand the effects. Vivid and subtle cases are likely to drive the point firmly into their mind.

Another policy recommendation for schools is that without exception each teacher should teach explicitly so that all students can understand the classroom work, assignments, and how they should be done. Teachers should teach to the success of all students, including African-American males. Moreover, all teachers should be required to give African-American males the grades they earn. And teachers who continually write referral notices on African-American males should be investigated by the principals. Upon the word of the teacher in her referral note, the African-American male is easily sent home for ten days or the rest of the semester. The disciplinarian, male or female, white or African-American, has no patience or respect for the student. Either he is not allowed to give his side of the incident that sent him to the office, in the first place, or he is neither "heard" nor "understood" while he attempts to explain what occurred.

Does dropping out of school result only from the student's behavior? Are African-American schools the answer? These are pertinent policy questions. The evidence in this book suggests that family, school, the criminal justice system, and students are responsible for African-American males dropping out of high school. Moreover, it suggests that African-American administrators are no more understanding than white administrators. This blatant white and African-American racism against young black teenagers needs to desist if we are to make the kind of men out of them they deserve to become. The social policy of any school system should incorporate a fair and equitable resolution of all problems. And in-school suspensions and special learning centers should be established for all males who have behavior problems. Thus, the need is not for African-American schools; the need is for schools that meet the needs of African-American males. All school systems should be capable of making and implementing such determination.

Because of tempers in the home and unequal treatment in the school, workplace, and criminal justice system, some African-American high school males are angry young men. They are in contact with each other and with their white peers which leads to experimentation with quick tempers that also causes them to be sent home. Social policy should incorporate student adjudication teams in each school that resolve the problems among African-American high school males and between African-American males and white males. By no means should African-American males be sent home for fighting. They belong in the classroom because the streets devastate them.

There are also policy recommendations for the African-American community. First and foremost, the African-American community organizations ought to establish a task force for each housing development in each high school. For African-American males, it should be their duty to investigate teacher referral notices, suspensions, expulsions, and intra-race and inter-race in-school behavior. That is, it should be the duty of a task force to see that justice is served in every school problem related to African-American males.

Then, there is much that the rest of the African-American community can do. All social and civic organizations, sororities, and fraternities should organize a club of 100 men. The 100 men clubs should include males 6 to 80. And in these meetings, what constitutes manhood should be the focal point--with emphasis on eliminating quick tempers and promoting a healthy attitude. Also, these organizations of 100 men should focus on healthy bodies, healthy minds, spiritual minds, honest money, honest work, and keeping their trousers zipped; unzipped trousers create but do not nurture--a message that should be ingrained in the mind of all African-American teenagers.

Another solution to quick tempers for males ages 10 to 24 is a Disc Jockey Outreach program. As leaders of communities across America, I encourage them to ask rap stars and other performers to make quality rap records that condemn quick tempers and compliment unflappability and send them to radio stations all over America. Ask the radio stations in each city to permit its disc jockeys to play these records regularly. Let the records be hip. Get the attention of the African-American male on his own territory-rap land. He loves rap! Let's give him what he likes, but change the message to change him. Help him to be cool by being no fool.

Community organizations should also hold racism seminars and teach African-American males how to deal with white racism from their school peers. Some white high school males antagonize some African-American males by failing to speak to them, calling them names, and standing up close to them in antagonistic poses with no apparent intention to fight. Their apparent intention is to get the African-American male sent home for life. That is, to give him a life sentence of no high school diploma. The result is that the African-American male reacts and strikes first. He gets suspended or expelled and the white male gets an education. In the racism seminars, the African-American male should be taught to report all adverse behavior of white males to the administration and teachers and tactfully but forcefully insist on justice.

Besides, community organizations should teach African-American males self control. When the young white male stands up in an antagonistic pose, the African-American male ought to know that it is more manly to walk away than to fight and lose an education. He doesn't know this. The leaders of the community must tell him before it occurs. When he learns what is going on and becomes a fighter for his own freedom, it will make a difference. When African-American males can not walk away from trouble, teach them to wait until the white male strikes. Let them know that white males are not going to hit them because they love school and fear their awesome blows.

Moreover, if the African-American male must get angry with his white peer, community organizations should teach him how to re-direct his anger. That is, tell him to get angry with his white peer for thinking he is stupid enough to fight and get suspended from school. And, instead of fighting, get so angry that he does everything right and succeeds. And let him know that --only then-- is he a winner. That's super anger! If they must get angry, tell them to get angry for their freedom! Freedom from suspensions and expulsions, freedom from temper, violence, drugs, and prison, and freedom from losing out on a high school diploma.

The findings in this study also suggest policy for African-American churches. The church is the oldest surviving African-American organization in the country and is duly equipped to solve the problems of African-American males. It can develop varied programs to save African-American males. First, African-American churches should have a Pulpit--Save the Black Male--Ministry. In these sermons ministers should preach what the African-American male needs to do to get rid of his quick temper; moreover, they need to send out the message each Sunday morning that African-American males are a deep well of potential that can be tapped for success if they get rid of their quick temper and develop a better attitude. This message should explain the nature of quick temper, how to overcome it, and the advantages of overcoming it. Besides, pulpit messages should tell African-American males they can become as successful as they desire. These messages should be empowered with scriptural references and be preached the way African-American males learn. The object is to use the message to give young men a new vision of themselves and their lives. Moreover, ministers, in their Sunday morning messages, should help African-American men forsake their temper and anger and give their lives to Jesus. This alone will solve the problems of African- American males.

Next, the ministers should come down out of their pulpits and, along with their church members and other volunteers, conduct a daily four hour tutoring ministry. African-American ministers should personally go into the housing developments and low rent housing areas with church members and other volunteers and get young males ages 6 to 18 committed to attend the tutoring program. The ministers must staff these programs with qualified individuals, including men. The African-American male's first stop after school should be the church and not the street corners, drug dealers, and basketball courts. The church should see that all African-American males are prepared daily for the next day's school work. This will make them forget about their quick temper and think about success in education. The angry African-American male is merely looking for success and prefers educational success to a quick temper. He only needs help to make the change.

Further, the churches and recreational centers in each American city should conduct summer classes in mathematics, English, reading, and writing and personally gather the males to attend. While teaching them subject matter, interject values and high morals. Teach the whole man and tempers will dissipate. If only fifty students are enrolled in each program that will make a difference in the achievement of African-American males.

Also, the church should sponsor weekly seminars on values and morals. Again, males ages 6 to 18 should be invited to these seminars. Change their values from a quick temper to quick learning. Give them a different value system. Further, the church and community organizations should sponsor seminars to teach parents how to rid their children of deceit about their school attendance and school work.

There are also recommendations for the African-American family. One of the problems is that African-American males often live with only one parent, the mother. Some mothers call their son baby when they ought to be teaching him how to become a man. Seminars should be made available for pregnant women and mothers with sons from birth to eighteen years to teach them how to rear their sons to become men.   Additionally, such seminars should teach mothers and fathers how to nurture their children from birth to age eighteen, which includes helping them with their homework. If they are unable to assist their children, it is their responsibility to ask neighbors and churches for help. Parents on all socioeconomic levels need to become actively involved in the academic life of their children. Implementation of these suggestions along with those on the federal, state, school, community, and church level will greatly improve the African-American male population.

Then, there are recommendations for African-American males. They should practice becoming achievers in school, in civic organizations, and in the church. For example, inner city African-American males have a great capacity for excelling in high school.   In other words, they should do well in all their courses.   During street life, they often think and act quickly to gain status, protect themselves, and survive. Hence, they have the ability to provide answers swiftly.   Because street life is an effective teacher, I believe that school teachers can teach those same males to understand classroom work. Transferral of quick thinking, analysis, and action to the classroom will reap enormous benefits for African-American males. They will not only stay in school and graduate, but they will also be more competitive with other students.

Moreover, they should work on their attitude and quick temper. Some African-American males need to improve their disposition, during childhood and young adulthood, and practice honest work. In addition, they should participate in the programs suggested here that are designed for African-American males. Hence, their goal should be to take advantage of all the programs suggested for policy with the notion of becoming responsible and achieving men. If the programs and self-help proposed here are implemented, a large number of African-American males, regardless of age, will stay in school, graduate, and go to college.

These policy recommendations are suggested for two reasons. To eradicate the problems of African-American males, the society that sustains the conditions of African-American high school males must change and the African-American males must change. Hence, the point that we make here is that these policy recommendations are intended to change society and the individual simultaneously. If external and internal factors are removed from the lives of African-American teenagers, they will stay in school, graduate on time, go to college, and make this a better America.

Bibliography

Armao, Rosemary, "Dear Guv: Here's how to keep us in school," The Virginian-Pilot , Dl, D4, October l, 1990.

Azcoitia, Carlos and Philip A. Viso, "Dropout Prevention Chicago Style," Vocational Educational Journal 62 (March 1987) pp. 33-34.

Bachman, Jerald G. and Elizabeth Van Diernen. Youth Look at National Problems, University of Michigan, Ann Arbor: Institute for Social Research, 1962.

Barnes, Annie S. Single Parents in Black America. Bristol: Wyndham Hall Press, 1987.

Bell, Derrick, "The Case for a Separate Black School System," The Urban League Review ll (Summer 1987), pp. 136-145.

Clark, Kenneth B. Dark Ghetto New York:Harper & Row Publishers, 1965.

Coleman, James S. and Thomas Hoffer. Public and Private High Schools. New York: Basic Books, Inc., Publishers, 1987.

Comer, James P., Beyond Black and White. New York: Quadrangle Books, 1972.

Comer, James P., "Racism and the Education of Young Children," Teachers College Record 90 (Spring 1989), pp.352-361.

Comer, James P. et al., "School Power: A Model for Improving Black School Student Achievement," The Urban League Review 7 (Summer 1987), pp.187-200.

Dent, David J., "Readin,' Ritin' & Rage," Essence 20 (November 1989), pp. 54-59, ll6, ll7.

Dubois, W. E. B. The Crisis, A Record of the Darker Races. New York. Negro Universities Press, 1969.

Dunham, Roger G. and Geoffrey P. Alpert, "Keeping Juvenile Delinquents in School: A Prediction Model," Adolescence 22 (Spring 1987), pp.45-57.

Edmonds, Ronald, "Effective Schools for the Urban Poor, "Educational

Leadership 37 (October 1979), pp. 15-24.

Fisher, Anthony Leroy, "The Best Way Out of the Ghetto, " Phi Delta Kappan 60 (November 1978), pp.240-241.

Foster, Herbert L. Ribbin' Jivin' The Dozens. Cambridge:Balling Publishing ing Company, 1986.

Garibaldi, Antoine M. and Melinda Bartley, "Black School Pushouts and Dropouts Strategies for Reduction," Urban League Review 11 (Summer 1987), pp. 227-35.

Gibbs, Jewelle Taylor (Ed.), "Conclusions and Recommendations" in Young, Black, and Male in America: An Endangered Species. Dover: Auburn House Publishing Company, 1988.

Gilbert, Shirl E.,II and Geneva Gay, "Improving Success in School of Poor Black Children," Phi Delta Kappan 67 (October, 1985), pp. 133-137.

Ginzberg, Eli. The Negro Potential. New York: Columbia University Press, Press, 1956.

Good, Thomas L., "Teacher Expectations and Student Perceptions: A Decade of Research, "Educational Leadership 39 (February 1981), pp. 415-421.

Hale, Frank W., Jr., "An Agenda for Excellence: You Can Make the Difference," Phi Delta Kappan 60 (November 1978), pp. 204S-206S.

Herenton, Willie W. "Memphis Inner-City School Improvement Project: A Holistic Approach for Developing Academic Excellence, "The Urban League Review 11 (Summer 1987), pp. 209-235.

Holland, Jerome H. Black Opportunity New York: Weybright and Talley, 1969.

Johnson, Roosevelt, Black Agenda for Career Education. Columbus, Ohio: ECCA Publications, Inc., 1974

Johnson, Charles S. Growing Up Black. New York: Schocken Books,1967.

Lee, Courtland C., "The School Counselor and the Black Child: Critical Roles and Functions" Journal of Non-White Concerns 9 (April 1982) pp. 94-101.

Lindsey, Paul and Ouida Lindsey. Breaking the Bonds of Racism. Homewood: ETC Publications, 1974.

Lyons, Nancee L. "Homogeneous Classes May Be Best Way to Curb Black Male Dropout Rate, " Black Issues in Higher Education 6 (January 1990), pp. 10-11.

Mack, Faite R-P.,"Understanding and enhancing self-concept in black children," Momentum 18 (February 1987), pp. 22-25.

Marockie, Henry and H. Lawrence Jones, "Reducing Dropout Rates Through Home-School Communication," Education and Urban Society 19 (February 1987), pp. 200-211.

Meier, August and Elliott Rudwick. From Plantation to Ghetto, Third Edition. New York: Hill and Wang, 1966.

Monaco, Fred and Philip Parr, "From Problems to Promise in Pittsburgh, " Vocational Education Journal 63 (September 1988), pp. 39-41, 52.

Moody, Charles D., Sr. and Christella D. Moody, "Elements of Effective Black Schools," The Urban League Review 11 (Summer 1987), pp. 176.

Norfolk Public Schools, Special Norfolk, Virginia High School Dropout Report, 1990.

Morgan, Harry, "How Schools Fail Black Children," Social Policy 10 (January/February 1980) pp. 49-53.

O'Keefe, Mark, "SAFE program is student's ticket to graduation," The Virginian Pilot D1, D4.

Patton, James M., "The Black Male's Struggle for an Education," in Black Men, Lawrence E. Gary (Ed.). Beverly Hills: Sage Publications, 1981, pp. 199-214.

Proctor, Samuel D., "A Mind Is A Terrible Thing to Waste," Phi Delta Kappan 60 (November 1978) pp. 201S-203S.

Reid, Ira De A. In A Minor Key: Negro Youth in Story and Fact. Washingington: American Council on Education, 1940.

Rosenthal, Robert and Lenore Jacobson. Pygmalion in the Classroom.New York: Holt, Rinehart and Winston, Inc., 1968.

Scott, Emmett, J. and Lyman Beecher Stowe. Booker T. Washington:Build-Builder of a Civilization. Garden City: Doubleday, Page and Co., 1917.

Strickland, William, "The Future of Black Men," Essence 19 (November, 1989), pp. 50-52, 110-114.

The Virginian-Pilot and The Ledger-Star "New schools designed for black males," September 30, 1990, Section D, Page D4.

Truby, Roy, "Home-School Projects That Work," Education and Urban Society 19 (February 1987), pp. 206-211.

United States Department of Commerce, "School Enrollment--Social and Economic Characteristics of Students," October 1988 and 1987. Washington: Bureau of the Census, April 1990.

Washington, Booker T. et al. The Negro Problem. New York: Arno Press, 1969, pp. 9-29.

Wiley, Ed, III, "Educators Call for Fairer, More Effective Means of Discipline in Schools" Black Issues in Higher Education 6 (January 1989), pp. 15-16.

Wolfstetter-Kausch, Heidi and Eugene L. Gaier, "Alienation Among Black Adolescents," Adolescence 16 (Summer 1981), pp. 571-485.

Woodson, Carter G. The Education of the Negro Prior to 1861. Washington: The Associated Publishers, Inc., 1919.

Woodson, Carter G.The Negro in Our History. Washington: the Associated Publishers, Inc., 1922.

Woodson, Carter Godwin. The Mis-Education of the Negro. Washington: The Associated Publishers, Inc., 1972

INDEX